PHILOSOPHY OF RELIGION SERIES

Editor's Note

The philosophy of religion is one of several very active branches of philosophy today, and the present series is designed both to consolidate the gains of the past and to direct attention upon the problems of the future. Between them these volumes will cover every aspect of the subject, introducing it to the reader in the state in which it is today, including its open ends and growing points. Thus the series is designed to be used as a comprehensive textbook for students. But it is also offered as a contribution to present-day discussion; and each author will accordingly go beyond the scope of an introduction to formulate his own position in the light of contemporary debates.

JOHN HICK

Contemporary Critiques of Religion

KAI NIELSEN

HERDER AND HERDER

1971
HERDER AND HERDER NEW YORK
232 Madison Avenue, New York 10016

Library of Congress Catalog Card Number: 72–170200
© Kai Nielsen 1971

Manufactured in Great Britain

Contents

Preface

Though my intellectual debts are manifold, as the reading of this book will make evident, my own thinking concerning religion grew out of youthful perplexities over the religion that most of us in the West are introduced to as participants. Later the classical philosophers (Greek, medieval and modern) increased this perplexity and still later Feuerbach, Kierkegaard and Nietzsche gave it a new dimension. Finally linguistic philosophers, both believers and sceptics, deepened the issues for me and enabled me to give my perplexities a more adequate formulation.

I am indebted to the editor of this series, Professor John Hick, for his criticisms of the manuscript, to Mr William Bean and to members of the department of philosophy at Brooklyn College for their criticisms of Chapter 5 and to the members (students and faculty alike) of the philosophy and religion departments of Rice University for their penetrating criticisms of an earlier version of my manuscript during the pleasant days of my visit to Rice.

Lastly I would like to thank my wife for her frequent labour with and careful criticism of *Contemporary Critiques of Religion*. The errors and oversights that persist are my own responsibility and remain for me a source of intellectual disquietude.

K.N.

The University of Calgary,
July 1970

1 Introduction

Many contemporary critiques of religion, and some counter-critiques as well, assume, as Feuerbach, Marx and Freud do, that the materialists and sceptics of the eighteenth century had successfully made out the intellectual case against religion. That religious belief persists in spite of this, they argue, is due to profound human needs rooted in the social and/or psychological conditions of human living (1).

I think these critics of religion are right. But whether I am right or wrong in such an assessment, to start by taking it as an assumption is surely a mistake in a fundamental critique of religion, for there are many able and sophisticated members of the intellectual community who do not believe that religion or even Christianity or Judaism is palpably false, unintelligible or incoherent. Rather they believe that belief has an intellectual ground to stand on — though indeed not only an intellectual ground — and that the standard critiques of religion inherited from the Enlightenment are themselves full of unjustified and indeed unjustifiable assumptions which can at least as rightly be claimed to be mythological as the claims of religion. It is to this prior intellectual issue that I shall turn. Indeed, such arguments in one form or another have gone on for centuries, though, as we shall see, there are some distinctive contemporary forms. But it is with such considerations that one should start (a) to have a meaningful dialogue between belief and unbelief, and (b) to start with what is conceptually fundamental.

If the critical case against religion can be sustained, then the kind of considerations raised by Feuerbach, Freud and Marx become very significant, as do the normative and psychologistic arguments — serving as religious counter-claims — about the need to believe. In such a situation, Pascalian or Jungian claims about the meaninglessness of life without God become significant, but without a prior agreement about the incoherence, or at least the utterly problematic quality, of belief in God, stress on such considerations cannot but seem to be a failure to go to the heart of the matter (2). So I shall try to get to what even a tolerably orthodox Jew or Christian or a man perplexed about the concept of God, e.g. 'Is belief in God really altogether "beyond belief"?', would take to be the heart of matter.

In discussing critiques of religion I shall limit myself to the fundamental religious conceptions of the Jewish-Christian-Islamic forms of life. It is not that I believe that these religions are superior to other religions, for in general I do not. I impose these limitations on myself simply because these are the religious forms of life that engage us and call forth our commitment or rejection. Our Western perplexity about, commitment to, or rejection of religion at least starts — and usually ends as well — with these religions. Sophisticated members of Jewish, Christian or Islamic confessional groups do not take religion to be a set of explanatory hypotheses. Their God is not a God of the gaps. Within such groups, to be religious is to have a consciousness of God and to make a resolute attempt to live on the basis of that consciousness. Integral to these traditions is the belief that 'God is real and that the whole universe is ultimately under the sovereignty and within the providence of divine love' (3).

It is here, however, where puzzlement about the very concept of God is acute. 'Providence', the benevolent guidance of God, no longer means for sophisticated believers that some supernatural reality, some creative source of all reality other than itself, is directing the scene so that we can discover in the ways things go the loving 'hand of God'. Natural disasters or moral calamities are no longer thought to call Divine Providence into question. No matter how things go or even conceivably could go, the non-Neanderthal Jewish or Christian believer is prepared to affirm the reality of God. But where the believer so uses 'God', conceptual perplexity arises. Suppose such a man says in anguish, 'O God, help me in my need'. There we are given to understand that he believes in God. But then his very discourse commits him to the belief that there are true and false statements concerning divinity, for, as Bernard Williams aptly puts it, 'to believe is

2

to believe *something*, and if there is anything that one believes, one ought to be able to say in some way — if not in the very narrow terms of sense-experience — what the difference is between what one believes being true and what one believes not being true' (4). Note that I have not in such a claim committed myself to verificationism but only to the common-sense point made by Wittgenstein in his 'Tractatus' that 'to understand a proposition means to know what is the case if it is true' (5). And to have such knowledge it is necessary but not sufficient to understand the meanings of the constituent terms of the sentence expressive of the proposition. But, to take an example relevant to our purposes, to understand the word 'God' as it is used in Jewish and Christian discourse, we must also understand what it would be like for 'God created man in his image and likeness' or 'In God alone man is sustained' to be true.

The catch is, however, that believers and non-believers alike, once they give up an anthropomorphic conception of divinity, do not understand — or so it would seem — what it would be like for such utterances to express true statements, or for that matter false statements. But in that case the very discourse of the believer lacks the kind of intelligibility requisite for Christian or Jewish religious belief.

Put just like that, such a claim has a dogmatic sound. Something more needs to be said about such a philosophical claim in order to make it quite evident *that* it is so and *how* it is so. Indeed, our central question is *whether* it is so. Where 'God' is taken to stand for a kind of mysterious cosmic superman who orders things one way rather than another, we have some rough idea what it would be like for it to be true or false that there is such a God. However, by now such religious belief has become idolatry. Such a God is (a) not adequate to the demands of the religious life, and (b) recognisably mythical. That is, we know that there is no such God.

However, such an utterly anthropomorphic Big-Daddy-in-the-Sky is plainly not the God of sophisticated theism; or at least it is not the image of God that asserts itself when such theists are thinking about the concept of God. Furthermore, while sophisticated believers agree with non-believers that there is no such cosmic superman, they do confess to

3

God and claim in all honesty to believe in a God which is not a Divine Object or Power transcendent to the world but is somehow either the mysterious ground of being and meaning or some necessary existent upon which everything else depends. But now we move from an intelligible but unacceptable concept of God to one which is at the very least problematical. A modern atheist takes such concepts of God to be so problematical as to be incoherent and unacceptable; a modern agnostic wonders if they have sufficient coherence to be, after all, just barely believable; and a sophisticated contemporary Jew or Christian believes these admittedly problematical and mysterious concepts to have enough intelligibility and coherence to provide the underpinning for a distinctive confessional group which is worthy of one's allegiance. To have established his case, a critic of religion must show that this last claim is not justified.

I shall attempt here to explicate and assess some of the major arguments directed towards that end; that is to say, I shall be concerned with a statement and assessment of some of the major arguments for sceptical postures towards the Judaeo-Christian tradition or towards any belief in God which bears a reasonably close family resemblance to a belief in the God of that tradition. I shall both critically examine the sceptical arguments of others and try to advance sceptical arguments of my own. It will be my aim, by taking certain responses of belief to unbelief, to create what in effect is a dialogue between believers and sceptics. There are indeed many critiques of religion and many defensive moves against these critiques. There is profundity as well as superficiality and clever silliness on both sides. (In a conceptual inquiry such as philosophy, both the clever silly and the man devoid of a sense of reality flourish. Sceptics and believers both have their share of each and sometimes an individual has both vices.)

I shall not attempt to catalogue all the different forms of belief and unbelief. Instead, I shall be concerned to examine what I take to be the most important critiques and responses to those critiques and then, as I remarked, to carry forth on my own in the context of this dialogue a critique of religion and theology. There are some evident and standing difficulties in such an approach. In my very selection of positions

4

and arguments for consideration there will be value judgements about which positions are most significant. To the extent that my value judgements here are idiosyncratic and arbitrary, such a selective approach will indeed suffer. Only if they are founded on an adequate judgement about what is central will such a selective approach be justified as anything more than a pragmatic measure to keep a slender volume from being a boring catalogue of names and digests of arguments. I have, of course, striven to make sensible and I hope perceptive value judgements here, but perceptive or not such a selective approach is necessary in a book of these dimensions.

When reflecting on such methodological considerations, we must not lose sight of the fact that when the contemporary religious scene is surveyed, it becomes readily apparent that what is religious belief for one man is idolatry for another, and sometimes for another no religious belief at all but a form of atheism or agnosticism or simply a metaphysical confusion. Radically different things on the contemporary scene pass for 'true belief' or 'true Christian faith' and the like. One man's belief is another man's atheism. What to take as 'true religion' or genuine Christian or Jewish belief is not evident. Often it is said that if religion is what a given critique of religion alleges it to be, then indeed that critique is a warranted critique of religion, but that all the same this critique is in reality trivial, for what has been criticised as religious belief is not a genuine or at least not a profound religious belief at all. It has been argued, for example, that Hume has convincingly shown that anthropomorphic conceptions of religion are unacceptable but that this is in reality a purifying aid to genuine religious belief, since such religious belief cannot treat God as an existent — even the superlatively best — among existents (6). What Hume intended — so the claim goes — as a devastating critique of religion actually serves to purify it by decisively refuting anthropomorphism.

It is difficult for a man who believes there is no such animal as 'true religion' to know what to do in such a circumstance, for no matter what views he criticises he can easily be accused of wasting his critical fire on some form of idolatrous belief and missing what is really essential to Christianity and Judaism. What are often called reductionist

5

analyses of religious belief seem more intellectually palatable to me than the more traditional analyses, but at the same time I share the traditionalist's conviction that these reductionist analyses in effect radically transform Christian and Jewish belief while purporting to be merely explicating it and that in this transformation much that has been traditionally taken as central has been abandoned (7). My strategy here will be to stick with what has traditionally been taken as doctrinally central in these religious traditions and to examine the case made against this traditional central core. There are able philosophers — masters of the most sophisticated analytical techniques — who think that the extant critiques of such traditional religious beliefs fail. Their rather massive cultural acceptance by the intelligentsia, such philosophers believe, attests to the fact that sceptics have their mythologies too, and that sometimes these gain intellectual currency. That this is often so is no doubt true, but I shall try to show that there are crucial contemporary critiques of religion which rest on no mythology.

II

In Chapters 2-4 I shall examine what I call empiricist critiques of religion — critiques stemming from the work of the logical empiricists — and the attempts to meet this challenge. In Chapter 5 I shall consider a very fundamental critique of religion at least seemingly inherent in the conceptual relativism of Wittgenstein and — though in a different way — of Quine. I shall attempt to show, contrary to those Wittgensteinian philosophers I have elsewhere characterised as Wittgensteinian fideists, that its implications in reality undermine Christian and Jewish belief (8). If conceptual relativism is true, religion should totter. Finally, in Chapter 6 I shall inquire, independently of a general theory or criterion of meaning or significance, whether the concept of God can be shown to be incoherent and thus an unacceptable concept. That is to say, I shall consider whether an examination of the very logic of 'God' in its non-anthropomorphic employments reveals that it has devastating conceptual incoherences.

6

There remain, before we turn to an examination of empiricist critiques of religion, several additional preliminaries that need attention.

1. The very title of this book, as well as my above remarks, will seem to some to betoken a confusion concerning what philosophy can legitimately do. Faithfully following Wittgenstein's methodological reminders and sharing his philosophical postures, D. Z. Phillips has — to take a striking example of this — contended that 'the whole conception of religion standing in need of justification is confused' (9). 'Philosophy', he continues, 'is neither for nor against religion, "it leaves everything as it is". This fact distinguishes philosophy from apologetics . . . It is a philosophical blunder of the first order to think that religion as such is some kind of mistake' (10).

Phillips is surely correct in maintaining that philosophy should not be — as sometimes it has been — a biased partisan advocacy either for or against religious belief. That is indeed a perversion of both philosophy and rationality. We have no need of that in philosophy. But at least the central portions of the work of Augustine and Aquinas, Spinoza and Hume and even the quite different work of Kierkegaard and Feuerbach cannot be justly accused of such biased advocacy. Yet Augustine's, Aquinas's and Kierkegaard's arguments serve to support Christianity and Spinoza's, Hume's and Feuerbach's to undermine it. Moreover, the central core of their arguments for belief or unbelief were indeed reasoned philosophical arguments and not propaganda or unphilosophical advocacy. That this is so surely shows that Phillips's remarks, if taken at their face value, are unjustified.

However, Phillips, or at least many Wittgensteinians, would reply that in speaking of 'philosophy' in such a context, they are referring to what we now recognise to be the proper office of philosophy since philosophy has taken a linguistic and analytical turn. I think we should be very cautious about that editorial 'we'. I like to think of myself as an analytical philosopher, but I would make no such claim concerning what philosophy can and cannot properly do and this would hold for many others as well. But orthodox Wittgensteinians regard anything other than description as an impurity in philosophy. Such a methodological stance is indeed understandable. It also combines easily with Barth's theological approach.

Barth has taught theologians to be sceptical about the claims of philosophy vis-à-vis Christianity. Christianity has little to do, where it is genuine, with philosophical activity and does not need the philosophers' imprimatur. Siding with this, James Cameron — also a philosopher of a Wittgensteinian persuasion — seeks, as does Phillips, to give this Barthian stance a philosophical rationale. Cameron remarks that 'most' "Western" philosophers would deny that it is their proper occupation to teach wisdom that could in any way be thought to rival Christianity. Very bold philosophers may be found to comment on the grammar (in Wittgenstein's sense) of theological statements, but that is all' (11).

However, the part about teaching wisdom aside, Cameron's statement is surely false, even for analytic philosophers, if taken for what it purports to be, namely a descriptive statement of fact. Surely Ronald Hepburn's 'Christianity and Paradox', C.B. Martin's 'Religious Belief', Antony Flew's 'God and Philosophy', and W.I. Matson's 'The Existence of God' are not, anthropologically speaking, philosophical freaks and they clearly are all squarely in the analytic tradition. Yet they do not only comment on the grammar of 'God' but also make forceful criticisms of religious conceptions. That their arguments may contain grave errors is entirely irrelevant to the present point. Terence Penelhum is far more accurate than Cameron or Phillips when he remarks of such a typical collection of analytical essays in philosophical theology as those in 'New Essays in Philosophical Theology' 'that the description of the religious use of words is not carried on without judgement of its legitimacy' (12).

I believe that Cameron would, if pressed, amend his remark by saying that it is not to be interpreted descriptively but to be taken as a remark about how philosophy, properly aware of its limitations and its distinctive role, should proceed. Taken in this way, Cameron's remark does characterise the work of some philosophers and does catch the methodological stance of many more.

Such an utterly neutralist approach I take to be mistaken, and fundamentally so, and yet it is a position which a

8

conscientious philosopher could easily be led to espouse. To begin to see why it is mistaken, it would be well to start with some remarks of D.Z. Phillips. There is, of course, irony in this, for, as we have seen, he argues for a neutralist position, but all the same he sometimes makes perceptive remarks which in reality help undermine his own professed position. He points out that where 'moral and religious beliefs are concered', one cannot correctly say 'that whatever answers are given in philosophy, the role which moral and religious beliefs play in people's lives goes on regardless' (13). Religion as we have it now is hardly philosophically innocent. People who have read any philosophy may, vis-à-vis religion, already have been indirectly affected by philosophy. Bad philosophy, Phillips argues, can give us a mistaken understanding of our beliefs, religious and otherwise, leading to 'the loss or an obscuring of religious understanding which might have been possible otherwise' (14). Phillips takes as an example 'the philosophical equation of immortality and survival, eternity and duration' (15). Many people give an account of their belief in the immortality of the soul in terms of 'survival after death'. If they come to learn something of philosophy and come to see that philosophy shows such account of immortality to be mistaken, they may come to believe that their 'faith has been shown to be mistaken too, whereas that is not the case' (16). It is also the case that there are people who, as a result of bad philosophy, 'only give an account of the immortality of the soul in terms of survival after death' and come to believe this so thoroughly that this is what their faith has come to be. What started out as an *account* of a belief became *the belief* and 'philosophy has contributed to the creation of illusions, dreams, which can never be realised, and hopes which can never be fulfilled — hopes of surviving death, of meeting loved ones again, of inheriting a better life beyond the grave where the misfortunes and deprivations one has suffered in this life are compensated in full' (17). Philosophy, he points out, can surely effect belief by showing that one cannot speak in a certain way, e.g. that it is senseless to speak of the survival of bodily death. But philosophy may also help us to come 'to see the possibility of speaking in another way' (18).

It is here that Phillips makes an important remark vis-à-vis

9

the alleged higher-order neutrality of philosophy. 'Now, here,' he asks, 'when one speaks of "coming to understand", "coming to see it as a possibility", "coming to see the point of it", is it easy to draw a sharp distinction between giving an account of the immortality of the soul, and believing in the immortality of the soul?' (19). He answers rightly that it is not and goes on to assert that sometimes 'in an individual's experience, coming to see the point of religious beliefs is at the same time the increase or dawning of philosophical and religious understanding. What I mean is that philosophical and religious understanding go together here. The deepening of philosophical understanding may at the same time be the deepening of religious understanding' (20). But then clearly philosophy — and good philosophy, too — can help justify religious belief, and if it can help justify religious belief it can also criticise it. A logical ban on one is also a logical ban on the other. And since they are complementary, one of the activities cannot be legitimate without the other being legitimate as well. If there is no ban for one there can be no ban for its complement either. Moreover, in lieu of a very extensive justification, it is the grossest form of biased advocacy to assert that 'good philosophy' justifies belief by deepening our understanding of how it must be a true account of the ultimate nature of things while 'bad philosophy' criticises religious belief.

2. In raising fundamental questions about the intelligibility and/or rationality of the alleged truth-claims of religion, there is no claim on the part of these critics of religion that religious discourse is flatly meaningless. 'God', 'redemption', 'sin', 'creation' and the like have a use in the language and there are deviant and non-deviant religious utterances that fluent speakers of the language, believers and non-believers alike, readily recognise. 'God is a good chair' is deviant; 'God is our loving Father' is not. Whatever trouble we may have concerning the latter's truth-value, we would not balk at it, though we would balk at 'God sleeps faster than Neptune' or 'Is loving God not Father a is'. Someone correcting proofs would under normal circumstances halt at the latter two but would go on without any hesitation at all with 'God is our loving Father'. Such considerations make it evident enough that we have some understanding of that discourse. It isn't

10

flatly meaningless.

However, the philosophically interesting question concerning its intelligibility turns around whether utterances such as 'God created the heavens and the earth' or 'Man is utterly dependent on God' actually are, as they purport to be and appear to be, genuine truth-claims. Is there something we can say about God which is factually informative and literally true? True in the same way or at least in a very similar way that statements about the external world are true? (21) Some may feel that this request is too strong. Perhaps what is literal and non-literal or even cognitive and non-cognitive cannot be so neatly divided (22). But what, at the very least, we do want to know is whether there can be any true religious beliefs, which in any reasonable sense are objectively justified. (I have in mind, of course, fundamental religious beliefs such as 'God created the heavens and the earth' and not beliefs such as 'Jesus was born in Bethlehem'.) The Christian faith, by contrast, has — as N.G.H. Robinson has maintained — always 'made a claim to finality, believing that it is the will of God that men believe on Him whom He hath sent and finding in Christ *the* way, *the* truth, and *the* life' (23). Judaism and Islam have made similar ultimate truth-claims (putative truth-claims). Our fundamental question is: Have the contemporary critiques of religion utterly undermined such religious claims or do they yet remain viable for a man who would, while remaining non-evasive, make sense of his ensnarled life?

3. As I remarked earlier, my approach is of necessity selective. Much that is ignored here can be justifiably ignored because it is either peripheral or deals with the *logically* secondary, though still central, question: Must man believe in what is a scandal to the intellect in order to make sense of his life? (I have tried to face this question — more accurately, cluster of questions — in my 'Ethics Without God' and 'The Quest for God'.) But there are also two questions which are indeed central to a fundamental consideration of religion which I do ignore, namely the problem of evil and the paradoxes of omnipotence. My reasons for ignoring them are (a) that I am less convinced than are many sceptics of the failure of the subtler attempts by such believers as Hick, Plantinga and Phillips to rebut sceptical challenges centring

11

around these problems, and (b) that whether they are or are not successful, if the kind of critique explained and defended in this essay is essentially sound, all discussion of theodicy or the paradoxes of omnipotence will be quite unnecessary (24).

2 The Challenge of Empiricism

For good or ill, there is in the industrially developed countries an ever-increasing degree of secularisation. This sometimes, but by no means in most instances, leads to securlarism as well. There may be less exaggeration than many people would surmise in Herman Tennessen's remark that 'atheism is extinct in the more advanced parts of the world — for lack of opposites. A serious atheist is considered in Scandinavia a slightly ludicrous bore' (1). There is characteristically with 'modern man' neither an ideologically articulate rejection of religious belief nor an affirmation of it either. It is not, as Marx and Engels or Dewey and Russell hoped, that men have become self-consciously secularist and have replaced a Jewish or Christian *Weltanschauung* with a secular one which offers an overall interpretation of existence. Rather than replacing Jewish or Christian *Weltanschauungen* with at least a prima facie more rational account of man, society and nature, what has generally resulted is that modern man has no such account at all: he is simply without an articulate set of overbeliefs. He is secularised without being a secularist and he lives without a critical ideological awareness. It is not that he is committed to or even in favour of some alternative set of far-ranging interpretative norms, but that religious talk seems to him to be beyond serious consideration. It is not that he explicitly repudiates religious beliefs but that by now they are regarded by him as rickety old antiques. These religious beliefs play an ever more minimal role in his daily intercourse and in his haphazard account of himself and others. Modern man in such societies is scarcely atheistic or agnostic. He is, rather, non-theistic. Religion hardly calls forth his loyalty or real assent and it is not an object of critical or even dogmatic dissent.

Indeed, the above is a hypostatisation of 'modern man' and

13

it may suffer from overstatement. There are modern men and modern men, and some of them are indeed deeply committed religiously. But my remarks do catch a very considerable bulk of people who have become in varying degrees secularised. In saying that they are secularised, I mean that in attempting to understand, explain or assess the occurrences in their lives and the conditions of their lives, they characteristically do not appeal to religious categories and they do not think in religious terms. The authority of religion for them has an ever-diminishing sphere. Being a Jew or a Christian is hardly a live option or even something they seriously think about. Where a nominal religious affiliation remains, it is something primarily ritual, linked with birth, death, marriage, coming of age, and closely associated with certain dates (Easter, the High Holy Days, and the like). It is not something which is mandatory or something, as with George Eliot, Joyce or Hägerström, which can only be broken with after a severe spiritual crisis. As John Bowden and James Richmond put it, 'it is no longer obvious to the great mass of our contemporaries that religion still has valid knowledge to offer; it is no longer obvious that the average Western man or woman is obliged to have a religious outlook upon life' (2). Secularisation — and I do not mean a doctrinaire secular humanism — can and often does cut deep enough to make such questions about religious options seem quaint rather than driving, heart-rending options with which a man must wrestle. Even the world of Kierkegaard and Weil can seem very distant and peculiar — something like a strange tribe's commitments — to some Western men. Science and common-sense observation show us what is the case and explain what is the case. There can be no serious question about knowing anything or perhaps even understanding anything about some alleged putative realm or dimension behind or beyond the universe. Fictional or purely ideational conceptualisations apart, there is only one sort or level of existence and this is to have a place in space-time (3).

To be sure, many people who have been thoroughly secularised would not articulate their unstated assumptions as I just have. This would seem to them far too doctrinaire and positive. They just do not think in terms of the supernatural or the transcendent. Scientific ways of thinking

14

and explaining are more prestigious and pervasive norms in their society. Like people in more determinately religious times, they merely do what in their cultural circle is done by the taste-setters; and in the educated subculture of contemporary Western culture, it consists, sloppily no doubt, in thinking in secular terms.

We should now — moving away from armchair sociology — consider the rationale (rationales) for this and the soundness of such rationales. They are no doubt many, but a crucial one going back to the Renaissance and gaining force in the eighteenth and nineteenth centuries is the increasing authority of science and of scientific modes of conceptualising and explaining. In science (or so the belief goes) we have found a far more objective and successful method of basing belief than we had ever had before. It is self-corrective and not ethnocentric and political. If we want to know what our world is like, it is to scientific modes of conceptualisation, description and explanation that we must turn. Here, and here alone, as Pierce put it, we have a reliable method of fixing belief.

However, *if* this is so and *if* it is so for all that concerns man, why is this? Sometimes a purely pragmatic validation is attempted. Scientific ways of fixing belief, it is claimed, are the only ones that stand up in practice. Religious beliefs and moral beliefs remain essentially tribal beliefs incapable of a genuine cross-cultural validation. To such a pragmatic claim, it is natural to reply that while there are several difficulties in objectively justifying religious and moral beliefs, nevertheless, attention to their very nature shows that we should not expect them to be scientifically validated. The scientific method, or at least the exclusive use of the scientific method, simply will not work here. Indeed, scientific ways of fixing belief are highly successful in their own domain. And in that domain there is no reasonable alternative to them. But if we are to understand in any proper manner the distinctive claims of morality and religion, we must go beyond such purely scientific ways of validating belief.

Empiricism enters the scene when it is replied, with Russell and Ayer, for example, that what cannot — in principle cannot — be known by means of science or common-sense observation (and, of course, logical deductions and inferences from such observational reports) cannot be known. A.J.Ayer, in his contribution to a recent 'What I Believe' series, starts his essay with the remark: 'I believe in science. That is, I believe that a theory about the way the world works is not acceptable unless it is confirmed by the facts, and I believe that the only way to discover what the facts are is by empirical observation' (4). If many a plain man, who is thoroughly secularised, could explain his basic ideological posture, he would put the core of it in a very similar way. The theory supporting this belief is some form of empiricism. When extended, as it is by empiricists, not simply to theories about how 'the world works' but to all accounts about what there is, such an account poses a problem for Judaeo-Christian belief or for any belief in what Ninian Smart calls 'religious entities' or for that matter 'states' such as nirvana (5). The question is whether this empiricist challenge is a devastating challenge to the claims of religion or whether empiricism itself is so myth-eaten as really to afford no serious challenge to the legitimacy of religious ways of conceptualising the world.

II

I must first characterise empiricism and then consider some perspicacious contemporary empiricist critiques of religion. To be an empiricist is to believe that all our knowledge and understanding of matters of fact — of what is the case — is and must be based upon or derived ultimately from experience. In gaining knowledge of his world or of himself, there is no way by which man can transcend the boundaries of what is at least in principle either directly or indirectly observable. They are limited by the bounds of sense in gaining a knowledge of what there is. This characterisation is of course vague and loose, but any attempt to make it more precise would lead to more specific senses of 'empiricism' that not all empiricists would subscribe to.

David Hume and John Stuart Mill are, of course, the classical sources and Hume's critique of religion is one of the most thorough and probing critiques ever made, but in this book I shall be concerned with contemporary critiques of

16

religion. Contemporary empiricists, far more than their predecessors, have been self-consciously concerned with questions of meaning and language — with articulating criteria for what can be significantly asserted or denied and with fixing the bounds of what can be rightly taken to be a truth-claim. Metaphysical speculations and utterances have been 'condemned not for being emotive, which could hardly be considered as objectionable in itself, but for pretending to be cognitive, for masquerading as something they were not' (6).

Religion should not be viewed simply as a metaphysical world-view but as a system of salvation, and Christianity in particular as a medium of God's redemption of man. But religions such as Christianity and Judaism do commit their adherents to the acceptance of certain metaphysical claims. Jews and Christians make (or at least presuppose) metaphysical statements in which God is referred to as transcendent, and Christians in addition refer to Jesus as God incarnate. Here we have putative truth-claims (utterances which allegedly are used to make statements which are either true or false) which are integral to Judaism and Christianity and which most contemporary empiricists believe are cognitively meaningless, without factual significance, or so indeterminate in meaning as to be incapable of making a genuine truth-claim.

It is surely not the case that all religious-talk is metaphysical-talk or that religion is simply transcendental metaphysics. 'Oh Lamb of God who taketh away the sins of the world' is plainly not a metaphysical statement. And being religious (among other things) involves making utterances of that type. Furthermore, it is a way of orienting oneself in the world; it is not simply a matter of assenting to certain metaphysical beliefs. But being a Christian, which is one way of being religious, also involves a real assent to what the believer thinks is a truth-claim. 'Oh Lamb of God who taketh away the sins of the world' could not even be understood — in anything more than a pictorial sense — unless certain metaphysical concepts are intelligible.

The argument of the kind of empiricist called a 'logical empiricist' or 'logical positivist' is that concepts such as God — when not, like Zeus, used utterly anthropomorphically —

17

are pseudo-concepts and utterances such as 'God created the heavens and the earth' are employed in their natural habitat to make pseudo-factual statements without literal significance. That is to say, they parade as truth-claims but fail to satisfy the conditions of genuine truth-claims. Such empiricists argue that all *a priori* statements are analytic — that is, true by definition as 'Puppies are young' is true by definition — and that all other literal statements must be at least in principle verifiable to be genuine statements. That is, as Ayer puts it in his own account of the *Wiener Kreis*, 'statements . . . to which no empirical observation could possibly be relevant, are ruled out as factually meaningless' (7). Ayer goes on to add, significantly — for this is often overlooked — 'the emphasis here is on the word "factually". It is not denied that language has other uses besides that of imparting factual information' (8). Religious utterances, such empiricists maintain, can, as key emotive or ceremonial utterances, have profound human importance. What is claimed is that they are not capable of stating facts or making genuine truth-claims.

III

Our initial task is to state and examine this critique of religion. I shall first state Ayer's case for it in his much abused 'Language, Truth and Logic'. I shall supplement Ayer's account here with (a) some remarks by H. H. Price in his 'Logical Positivism and Theology' written at about the same time as 'Language, Truth and Logic' but independently of it, and (b) some closely related arguments, again in the empiricist manner, made about twenty years later by Braithwaite and Flew (9). I should add that Price and Braithwaite are empiricists who believe they can give a minimal account of Christian belief which will save it from incoherence. But in separating out what they take to be the precious kernel from the chaff, they offer critical arguments much in the manner of the logical empiricists and it is with these arguments that I shall be concerned in the present chapter.

Ayer's much discussed and much criticised account commences mildly enough (10). He remarks that it is now generally agreed that what Jews and Christians call 'God' can neither be demonstratively proved to exist nor do we have good inductive arguments which would justify our asserting that there probably is such a reality. Here, along with Price and Braithwaite and nearly everyone else who has examined the subject closely, he is on safe and rather uncontroversial ground. I do not mean to suggest that some able philosophers have not reopened these questions, for they have, but they are very much in the minority and their arguments have been forcefully contested (11). Indeed, it seems to be that it is more accurate to say 'devastated', but no such strong claim needs to be made here. It is sufficient to say that here Ayer, Price, Braithwaite and Flew are on well-tried ground and that the burden of proof is certainly on the theologian or philosopher who resists to show that there is some sound argument, deductive or inductive, for the existence of God. The arguments that have been offered have been refuted and there are thus at least prima facie good grounds for the claim that no reliable reasoning of such a type could be given.

There are, however, many sophisticated Jews and Christians who positively rejoice in the failure of such attempted proofs (12). Belief in God, they tell us, is a matter of faith, not of knowledge. Moreover, it has been argued by the more moderate fideists that it is reasonable to continue to believe in God purely *de fide* (13).

However, in a manner that would cut against such a fideism as much as against traditional natural theology, our three empiricist philosophers stress that there is a logically prior question that should plague a fideist as well as a more rationalistic Christian or Jew trying to render viable some form of natural theology. What is involved here can be brought out in the following way. All but the most Neanderthal of Jews and Christians have long ago decisively rejected a concept of God in which God, like Zeus, is thought of as being physically detectable and as having some spatio-temporal location. The concept of God which is now embedded in the Jewish-Christian tradition is, as Ayer puts it, a concept in which God is taken to be a transcendent being. But what needs to be faced by the fideist who would accept such a God on faith, or the natural theologian who would try

19

to find evidence for such a personal Creator of the world, is whether religious propositions of the type 'There is a personal God who created the world' or 'There is a transcendent World Ground to whom all things may be referred' are either true or false. Where religious claims, as is usually the case, are taken to be truth-claims, it remains true, as Braithwaite puts it, that unless 'this latter question can be answered, the religious statement has no ascertainable meaning and there is nothing expressed by it to be either true or false' (14). Such religious claims most certainly appear to be putative statements of fact — grand cosmological claims about the nature of the universe. And this is how Jews and Christians construe their beliefs about them. But how their construal can be correct in the case of fundamental bits of God-talk is not evident.

In such a situation, 'an examination of the methods of testing the statement for truth-value is' — as Braithwaite puts it — an essential 'preliminary to any discussion as to which of the truth-values — truth or falsity — holds of the statement' (15). It is, as we have seen, the claim of logical empiricists that such absolutely central God-talk is in reality without truth-value in spite of the fact that such talk contains key utterances which are ostensibly used to make truth-claims. In the religious discourses of Jews and Christians which are acceptable to even the tolerably educated faithful of such confessional groups, 'God' is what Ayer calls a metaphysical term, and since this is so it cannot be even probable that God exists. It cannot be even probable, Ayer contends, 'for to say that "God exists" is to make a metaphysical utterance which cannot be either true or false. And by the same criterion, no sentence which purports to describe the nature of a transcendent god can possess any literal significance' (16). A metaphysical utterance, on Ayer's account, is an utterance which purports to make assertions concerning what the metaphysician takes to be a reality which transcends the phenomena about which scientists can make generalisations and observations. Metaphysical utterances indeed have emotive and pictorial meaning, but supposedly they also are used by metaphysicians to make truth-claims — true or false literal assertions. But metaphysicians do not succeed in making truth-claims when they use such utterances. The

20

gravaman of Ayer's case against metaphysical utterances is that while purporting to be used to make literal assertions of fact, they are not made in accordance with 'the rules which any utterance must satisfy if it is to be literally significant' (17). What is taken to be the class of metaphysical statements is perhaps brought out with greater simplicity by Price (following a suggestion of Ryle) when he defines 'meta-physics' as 'the attempt to prove or disprove existential propositions which can neither be verified nor refuted by perceptual or introspective experience' (18).

Ayer makes it plain later, and no doubt this was also Price's intent, that 'verified nor refuted' should be construed liberally to mean 'neither directly nor indirectly confirmed or infirmed'. To assert that there is a saving creator and sustainer of the world or that God's purpose for man is shown in the providential ordering of the universe is to engage in God-talk which is also metaphysical-talk, and while on occasion this metaphysical-talk is emotively potent, it is nevertheless nonsensical, i.e. it is without literal significance. Such talk purports to express propositions but fails. Its significance is only emotive.

God is conceived of as a person or agent who is omnipotent, omniscient, morally perfect and an utterly incorporeal, non-spatio-temporal reality, but, Ayer remarks, 'the notion of a person whose essential attributes are non-empirical is not an intelligible notion at all. We may have a word which is used as if it named this "person" but, unless the sentences in which it occurs express propositions which are empirically verifiable, it cannot be said to symbolise anything' (19).

When a religious believer claims he is expressing genuine propositions as he engages in religious activity — activity involving discourse which presupposes such an allegedly transcendent reality — he in reality does not succeed in saying anything about the world, and thus he cannot justly be accused of saying anything false or anything for which there are insufficient grounds. If we remove all reference to what is in any way experienceable (directly or indirectly), our putative factual statements cannot even be false, and in that case we cannot correctly say anything which is true, probably true, or even reasonable to assert. We may be expressing and evoking our emotions — our fundamental attitudes about life — or in an oblique and misleading way telling people how to act or what attitudes to take towards life, but we have not even obliquely succeeded in making a truth-claim. It is, Price observes, 'natural to assume that theological statements are *not* verifiable, nor of course refutable by experience'. And if this is so, they are indeed nonsensical and quite incapable of being believed or doubted, for there is nothing to be believed or doubted. 'You cannot be uncertain whether God exists or not if there is no such question' (20). Price rightly adds, accounting for what looks like the contradictory claim that people believe in what is unbelievable, that it is of course 'possible to believe *that a statement makes sense*, though one cannot *see* for oneself that it does. . .' (21). This belief is an empirical belief, and like all empirical beliefs it can be false. In the case of God-talk, such a belief, empiricist critics maintain, is false, for a statement is factually significant only if it is verifiable, and if putative statements such as 'God exists' are not verifiable then the 'statement that God exists is nonsensical, and whatever it may express, it cannot possibly express belief in the existence of its grammatical subject: no more than "virtue is blue" can express a belief about virtue. That which is nonsensical cannot possibly be believed. (We are, of course, still assuming that no statement about God can be experientially verified or refuted.) Thus, when a man says he believes that God exists, he cannot possibly mean what he says' (22).

IV

However, has it really been established that such non-anthropomorphic bits of putatively assertive God-talk are utterly unverifiable? When talking about prima facie factual statements, Price remarks, much as would Ayer, that 'if verifying a statement means experiencing something, which makes it certain or probable that the statement is true, then the Principle of Verifiability is both true and important. . .' (23). And in talking about existential statements (statements stating particular matters of fact), Price also asserts that if 'we do not know what sort of entities we must be acquainted with in order to verify a given statement, then it seems to me obvious that we are not talking sense when we utter the statement' (24). But 'There is a God', 'There is an omniscient, omnipotent being', or even 'There is an eternal, uncreated, omnipotent, and omniscient, unique, infinite, personal Spirit who has created out of nothing everything other than himself' seem at least all to be existential statements and even in some sense seem to be assertive of a particular matter of fact. The claim of the logical empiricists is that they must then (in the sense characterised) be verifiable to be factually significant or to make a literal truth-claim. But how can we be as confident, as Ayer and Braithwaite are, that they are not verifiable?

Some remarks of Braithwaite's are helpful here: 'There are three classes of statement whose method of truth-value testing is in general outline clear: statements about particular matters of empirical fact, scientific hypotheses and other empirical statements and the logically necessary statements of logic and mathematics (and their contradictories)' (25). He then proceeds to argue, as does Ayer, though less clearly, that religious statements of the appropriate genre are not verifiable in any of these ways and that no further way has been specified in which they are verifiable.

Suppose we take what Price believes to be the only feasible way for an empiricist to try to avoid assenting to the logical positivist claim that religious utterances are without truth-value. That is to say, suppose we argue that through religious experience we can verify or refute putative God-statements (26). If this is taken to mean that the prima facie statements in question state particular empirical facts which are testable by direct observation, then Braithwaite in effect argues that Price is plainly mistaken in making this suggestion, for if in a self-authenticating experience God can be observed, en-countered, met, then ' "God" is being used merely as part of the description of that particular experience' (27). Moreover, even if we drop the qualification about 'self-authenticating experience', we are still in intolerable difficulties, for it is a kind of category mistake to claim that God could be literally observed or encountered. Any reality that could be so detected would not be the God of developed Judaeo-

Christianity. As Braithwaite puts it, 'Any interesting theological proposition, e.g. "God is personal", will attribute a property to God which is not an observable one and so cannot be known by direct observation' (28).

The soundness of this objection is not affected by whether the religious experience is mystical experience or the more common variety of religious experience in which, through ordinary perception and introspection, we are thought by many believers to become aware of God's providence and his unique mode of causation. Mystical experience is allegedly an experience 'wholly different from ordinary sensing and introspection' and there may very well be such a kind of experience or indeed kinds of experience, but the point remains that no matter how it is experienced, if something can be literally experienced as located in space-time, it cannot − logically cannot − be God, i.e. an infinite, utterly transcendent, non-spatio-temporal reality.

It is more plausible to maintain that our key declarative God-talk utterances have the same status as or a very similar status to scientific hypotheses, and are verifiable (confirmable or infirmable) in the way they are verifiable. In an advanced science such as physics, we have, as Braithwaite points out, 'concepts of a high degree of abstractness and at a far remove from experience'. An electric field of force or a Schrödinger wave-function is no more directly observable than God. They are theoretical concepts whose meaning is given 'by the place they occupy in a deductive system consisting of hypotheses of different degrees of generality in which the least general hypotheses, deducible from the more general ones, are generalisations of observable facts' (29). Since this obtains for scientific hypotheses and their admittedly meaningful theoretical concepts, it is, Braithwaite concludes, 'no valid criticism of the view that would treat God as an empirical concept entering into an explanatory hypothesis to say that God is not directly observable' (30).

There are, however, Braithwaite argues, crippling difficulties in construing 'There is a God who created and sustains the world' and propositions of that order as explanatory scientific hypotheses or as having a logical status closely parallel to such hypotheses. If theological propositions are the same as or tolerably like scientific

24

hypotheses, then they must be refutable by experience. 'We must be willing to abandon them if the facts prove different from what we think they are. A hypothesis which is consistent with every possible empirical fact is not an empirical one' (31). Moreover, the theoretical concepts (theoretical under the present interpretation), e.g. God, redemption, providence, the soul, must be related to some but not all the possible events in the world to be non-vacuous. But consider 'If there is a personal God, how would the world be different than if there were not? Unless this question can be answered, God's existence cannot be given an empirical meaning' (32). That is, for our basic religious concepts to be genuine theoretical concepts, we must be able to answer that question. If declarative-mood God-talk is to have such a logical status, we must be able to say what it would be like for it to be the case that there is no God. It must, for example, be possible to describe the specific ways in which, if the course of history had been different, it would have been the case that God would not have existed — that is, eternally not have existed, for it is a grammatical remark to say that God timelessly exists if he exists at all. He could not cease to exist or begin to exist.

Antony Flew, in a much discussed brief symposium-piece, has developed this falsification argument into something which has been dubbed Flew's challenge (33). In response to questions like Braithwaite's about what the believer would take as a refutation of his claims, Flew points out that sophisticated believers use God-talk so that no conceivable states of affairs seem to count against their claims. If a sophisticated believer says 'God loves us as a father loves his children', he continues to hold that no matter what obtains. It does not function at all in these crucial respects like 'The Pope loves his cardinals'. No matter what happens — concentration camps, mass starvation, children wracked with cancer, endless exploitation and degradation of the poor — a Jew or a Christian continues to affirm 'God loves us as a father loves his children'. If we use the method of challenge on the believer and ask him what would you take — if it were to occur — as a refutation or as a disconfirmation of your claim, he cannot say what he would take as a dis-confirmation. And many would even regard the question and

B

25

the challenge as irrelevant. But this clearly shows that 'God' does not function like a theoretical concept in an explanatory hypothesis. Such religious propositions are not empirical hypotheses.

Flew, I should add, goes on to make a more sweeping challenge, which would put in question the very assertive status of such God-talk. To assert something is the case, Flew points out, is necessarily equivalent to denying that something is not the case (34). If someone utters 'p' and we are perplexed as to what 'p' means, one way of trying to find out at least what the user means by 'p' is to find out what he would regard as counting against or as being incompatible with the truth of assertions he makes in using 'p', for if such utterances are indeed assertions, they will necessarily be equivalent to a denial of the negation of them (35). Anything which would count against such an assertion must be part of what is intended (or at least what is implied) when its negation is asserted. 'If there is nothing which a putative assertion denies there is nothing which it asserts either: and so it is not really an assertion' (36). Thus, Flew continues, if it is not possible to say what would count against the assertion 'God loves us as a father loves us' and similar bits of God-talk, they are in reality pseudo-factual bits of discourse, i.e. bits of talk which appear to be assertive, appear to be factually significant, but actually only masquerade in this role. To show that such talk really has the requisite kind of intelligibility, it must be possible to specify what conceivable event or series of events, if they were to occur, would constitute 'a disproof of the love of, or the existence of, God'. It is a claim of logical empiricists that where the concept of God is used non-anthropomorphically, nothing does or could, and that thus such God-talk is devoid of factual content.

Braithwaite briefly considers a third way in which we might attempt to show that declarative God-talk succeeds in making an intelligible claim. Perhaps such religious propositions 'resemble the propositions of logic and mathematics in being logically necessary' (37). With the statements of logic and mathematics we have non-empirical statements but we still have a determinate method for establishing the truth-value of these statements. Why could not something similar hold for religious propositions? If it did, we would have solved our perplexity about their meaning by showing that, after all, they do make a truth-claim, though not an empirical truth-claim, but still a kind of truth-claim that modern empiricists find legitimate.

Braithwaite argues, as does Ayer, that if 'God exists' is logically necessary, it would follow that it makes 'no assertion of existence'. Hume and Kant, he remarks, have conclusively shown that 'no logically necessary proposition can assert existence' (38). Logical empiricists have argued that this is so because all such propositions are tautologies. But Braithwaite points out (as has Findlay as well) that it is not necessary to accept this controversial contention in order to make the claim that no logically necessary propositions assert existence. To see that this is so, it is only necessary to appreciate the force of the Humean-Kantian point that logically necessary propositions are essentially hypothetical. We need to remember that $4 + 2 = 6$ makes no assertion about there being any things in the world. What it says is that if there is a class of six things in the world, then this class is the union of two mutually exclusive sub-classes, one comprising four and the other two things. Similarly, if I assert 'Bachelors are unmarried', I do not commit myself to asserting that there are any bachelors or unmarried persons at all. I only commit myself to the claim that if there are bachelors, they are unmarried. And when I assert 'There are no married bachelors', I do not assert the existence of any person or object or give you to understand that some concept has instances. Rather, I give you to understand that the concept of married bachelor is one that could not possibly have any instances, since it is a self-contradictory notion. Thus, if 'God exists' were what it surely appears not to be, namely, a logically necessary proposition, then it is also an utterance which fails to do what it must do for it to have the role believers require it to have in their particular religious form of life — namely, to assert the existence of something. (This form of life, note, is distinctive of traditional Judaism and Christianity.)

Alternatively, it may be asserted that God's existence must be in some sense or other necessary, for to assert that God exists is surely to assert that a being exists who could not

27

cease to exist or come to exist, and thus if there is such a reality it in some sense must have necessary existence. But if this is so, Braithwaite replies, it still remains the case that 'no method has been provided for testing the truth-value of the statement that God is a necessary being, and consequently no way given for assigning meaning to the terms "necessary being" and "God" ' (39).

V

The empiricist challenge then comes to this. God-talk of the appropriate type is taken by its users to make truth-claims. These (at least) putative truth-claims are indeed of profound importance since they purport to assert an ultimate order of fact, e.g. 'God shall raise the quick and the dead' or 'There is an eternal reality upon whom the world depends'. But a statement only has factual significance if it is at least verifiable (confirmable or infirmable) in principle, and where we are asserting the existence of some particular matter of fact — such as God ('The infinite individual' or 'Unconditioned Transcendent' or 'The Maker of the World') allegedly is — then it must be the case (as Price puts it) that 'to know the meaning of such a statement must certainly *include* knowing what sort of entities we must be acquainted with in order to verify it. . .' (40). But the word 'God' seems plainly to be used in such a way that nothing could count as observing or taking note of (as taking note of a pain) God (41). Surely Ninian Smart is on safe ground when he asserts that 'from quite early times the central concepts of religion, such as God and nirvana, already include the notion that the entity or state they stand for cannot literally be observed. It would be a kind of category mistake to say that nirvana can be detected by radio or that the Father can be seen in a telescope' (42). It follows that there can be no experiencing God or encountering God or being aware of the presence of God, if that talk is to have any straighforward meaning. And so the conceptual perplexity concerning our understanding of 'God' becomes acute. For after all, what would it be like to verify that there is a God or a transcendent reality who will afford us eternal life? As we have seen — or so the empiricist challenge runs — such putative truth-claims are utterly

28

unverifiable and thus are devoid of literal meaning; that is, they are not intelligible factual assertions. Believers mistakenly believe them to have such a factual status. Indeed, for Christianity and Judaism to be what they have been, they must assume them to have such a status (43).

Price rightly points out that one can indeed believe that a statement makes sense even though one does not know what it means. 'Thus a pious but uneducated Christian would assume without question that the statement "God is both transcendent and immanent" makes sense, and that theologians can understand it; though he would not himself profess to know what it means. . .' (44). Thus, God-talk can be without literal meaning and yet Jews and Christians could quite consistently believe that it has literal meaning. They mistakenly think they believe in God when all they actually have is certain affective dispositions and the belief that certain religious authorities know what they are talking about. They believe that certain bits of God-talk have a literal meaning: that they can be used to assert an ultimate order of fact. But they are mistaken in this belief. That is to say, their meta-belief about religious discourse is mistaken and can be seen to be so on empirical grounds. Such key religious utterances are, it is maintained, not really factually assertive at all, but are either, as Ayer believes, purely expressive or evocative or, as Braithwaite believes, primarily expressions of our intentions, which we associate with certain stories which we at least entertain. But in either event, they are not truth-claims and they make no assertions about the nature of reality which may or may not be believed. But if they only have this non-cognitive kind of meaning and it is recognised that this is their only meaning, they may indeed be seen to square with empiricist theories of meaning and knowledge but they will, on such an interpretation, not meet the expectations that believers entertain about their beliefs (45). And those believers who accept such a reductionist account of their de-mythologised religious beliefs will have in effect undermined their religion by radically reducing its claims to something substantially but not verbally identical with a quite unequivocal form of atheism. As Flew puts it, such a form of religious belief will not be 'properly orthodox or practically effective' (46). Christian and Jewish preconceptions about their putative religious beliefs require them to construe their key declarative bits of God-talk as truth-claims about an (alleged) ultimate order of fact, but on such a construal their talk can be shown to be devoid of the appropriate kind of meaning required by their own expectations. In fine, belief requires that we construe them as truth-claims, but analysis shows that 'God created the world' or 'There is a God' are pseudo-factual statements without a literal meaning. Thus they cannot be genuine truth-claims. This is a central and perhaps the central challenge to religion of contemporary empiricism.

3 Rebuttals and Responses:I

The type of empiricist critique adumbrated in the last chapter has been much criticised. It is the conviction of many theologians, and a goodly number of philosophers as well, that such an empiricism foists on us an arbitrary and dogmatic criterion of meaning and that it simply rules out theological utterances as being devoid of literal intelligibility by arbitrary definitional fiat. Such an unempirical empiricism, it has been claimed, in reality constructs a secularist saving myth. The reality here is the fabrication of a myth for secular man, though the intent is merely to engage in conceptual analysis. But neither conceptual analysis nor any variety of careful philosophical reasoning should commit one to such a dogmatic and unjustifiable criterion for what it makes sense to say. This attitude towards such an empiricism is common enough and I shall in this chapter and the next attempt to state the core of the case against empiricist critiques of religion and then to examine what, if anything, remains of this empiricist critique.

There are several preliminaries that first need to be attended to. Logical empiricism or logical positivism, as it is sometimes called, is stone dead (1). Many of its leading representatives, including Ayer, are still very active philosophically, but they have so modified their positions that they no longer hold the iconoclastic position that was so distinctive of, and to many so philosophically liberating about, logical empiricism. Be that as it may, it is still the case that logical empiricism in certain respects at least made a definite advance over traditional empiricism. Prior to the development of logical empiricism, empiricists had not been able to account adequately for logical necessity and thus empiricism seemed quite evidently broken-backed. To try to construe the truths of logic and mathematics as empirical statements in principle open to empirical confirmation and disconfirmation will not do since it plainly will not account for their necessity. The logical empiricist stepped in here and accounted for the necessity of the statements of logic and mathematics by showing (or at least so they and many others thought) that they are analytic, i.e. true by definition and that their analyticity rests on our linguistic conventions. All *a priori* statements, they argued, are analytic and all other cognitively meaningful statements are at least in principle verifiable. The other uses of language, they argued, are all non-cognitive. Analytic statements tell us nothing about the nature of reality but reflect our determination to use symbols in a certain manner, e.g. that we use 'puppy' in such a way that it is equisignificant to 'young dog'. But that puppies are young dogs tells us nothing about our world beyond certain linguistic facts about our use of 'puppies'. All statements which are informative about the nature of our world are verifiable statements; non-analytic unverifiable utterances are cognitively meaningless.

Such is the core of logical empiricism. Few philosophers today would subscribe to all this core doctrine. It is particularly evident that there are meaningful utterances, indeed, cognitively meaningful utterances, perfectly literal and quite informative, which do not even purport to be verifiable. Moreover, some of them are not in the slightest degree emotive. 'Pass the butter', 'The witness must answer the question', 'Shoes worn in the rain should be polished', 'What time is it?', 'Be at the boat train at four', 'When in a slide do not apply the brakes' are plainly meaningful, cognitive (unless we stipulatively redefine 'cognitive'), literal, and they can readily function informatively in perfectly natural discourses. Such counter-examples show that the verifiability criterion of meaning could not possibly — except by arbitrary stipulations — serve as a general criterion of meaningful discourse or even a general criterion to sort out which utterance are cognitively meaningful or have literal meaning.

Moreover, unless we already understood an utterance — that is, unless it were intelligible to us — we could not even tell whether or not it was verifiable. For I must first understand 'p' to know what, if anything, would verify it. Knowing what 'Heidelberg is situated on the Neckar' means and what 'Visit Heidelberg' means, I know that the first utterance is used to make a verifiable statement, while the latter — perfectly meaningful — utterance does not so function. Furthermore, with 'You must not go to South

32

Germany without visiting Heidelberg' we have a perfectly literal, perfectly meaningful statement. But while that is evident, it is far from evident whether it is a verifiable statement. Such considerations clearly show that meaning is logically prior to and distinct from verification and that the meaning of a statement is not its method of verification. Only if we know what a statement *means*, can we know whether it is verifiable and, if so, how it is to be verified. Moreover, it is sentences and utterances which are meaningful or meaningless, and not statements; and it is statements, not sentences, which are true or false, literal or non-literal. Questions of meaning and verification should be kept distinct.

There are three further ways in which many logical empiricists went wrong, namely, in (a) their phenomenalism, (b) their stress on the priority of *ostensive* definition over all other forms of definition, and (c) in their remarks about conclusive verification.

I shall comment on (c) first. To say that a statement is only meaningful if it is conclusively verifiable or conclusively falsifiable is plainly too strong, for it would commit us to judging many utterances to be without literal meaning or factual significance which empiricists and non-empiricists alike recognise to be meaningful. (A) 'All live eels, not held in captivity, return to the sea from fresh water', (B) 'There is a man somewhere with three ears', and (C) 'Every book has some misprints', all, on such a criterion, must be judged to be literally meaningless. (A) is not conclusively verifiable since we cannot examine all eels. In fact, we do not even know what it would be like to have examined all the eels there are, now and in the future and literally everywhere. We do not even know what would count as having examined a fair sample of them. (Are there eels on Neptune?) By contrast one single good observation could conclusively verify (B), but nothing would conclusively falsify it. How do we know for certain — biologically improbable as it is — that somewhere at some time there is not some one with three ears? For all I know, perhaps there is. At any rate, we cannot be certain that there is not. And, finally, (C), in turn, shares the vices of both (A) and (B). As a universal statement it is not conclusively verifiable, and since we only spoke of 'some

33

misprints', we could never conclusively falsify it either, for we could not be sure that in some book somewhere there was not a misprint no matter how carefully we searched. But (A), (B), and (C) — practically and humanly trivial as they are — still are all utterances which are factually informative. Thus we cannot rightly say that a statement has literal meaning or has factual significance (has factual content) only if it is conclusively verifiable and/or conclusively falsifiable.

The problems about phenomenalism and the problems about ostensive definition are closely interrelated. Questions about meaning provoke fundamental questions about the relation of language to reality. How do we link our language to fact, how do we confront the world with our words so that they are not merely empty symbols?

Phenomenalism is the claim that 'statements about *the material* world are entirely reducible to statements about *sensa* actual and possible. . .' (2). To talk about tables and chairs, rainbows and fogs, pains and tickles, is to talk about sense-experiences actual and possible. To talk (assuming we are speaking English) about the brown shoe in the cellar or the fog over the castle is, among other things, usually to use such referring expressions as 'fog', 'castle', 'brown' and 'shoe', and these words — phenomenalists claim — in reality stand for sense-experiences actual or possible. That is what we are really talking about when we use such terms. And their meanings — now making the link with (b) — can only be learned by ostentation (by having the impressions for which they stand brought home to us). That is, we learn what a word means by having its referent (what it stands for) pointed out to us or otherwise non-verbally indicated, and this really consists in showing what sense impressions (our only direct objects of acquaintance) the word stands for.

However phenomenalism has failed, for no one has ever been able to produce one sense-data statement which is equivalent to a physical object statement. Moreover, if phenomenalism were true, we each would be caught up in a kind of solipsistic universe, each with his irreducibly private experience and his 'private language'. But language as a category of culture is clearly public, and though each person of necessity can have only his own experiences — in that way experiences must be private — the type of experience he has

34

need not be and hardly ever is utterly unique to him.

Phenomenalism was an entirely understandable attempt to get at what is simply given in experience: what, when symbolised, is that which reflects a direct correspondence between language and fact. In claiming that descriptive terms are meaningful only if they are ostensively definable, empiricists are working with a model of language which depicts language as being in a direct relationship with reality, e.g. meaningful descriptive terms stand in a 'Fido'-Fido relationship with what they symbolise. A word, syncategorematic terms such as 'and', 'if', 'then' and the like apart, is meaningful only if there is a correspondence — 'Fido'-Fido like — between word and object, and to know that there is such a correspondence or to know what would constitute such a correspondence is to know how the word in question — let us call it an object-word to distinguish it from syncategorematic words — is ostensively defined. In short, meaningful words are either syncategorematic words or object words and a word is a genuine object-word only if it is possible ostensively to define it: to point to the sense-experiences it stands for. With ostensive definition, we have the direct confrontation of words with what they allegedly mean, i.e. stand for, and we can in this way come to know if they really mean anything, for if they are not syncategorematic words and nothing specifiable counts as their referent, then they are not meaningful: they are just marks symbolising nothing. Moreover, while sentences are indeed not just lists of words — there is such a thing as syntax — sentences cannot simply be made up of syncategorematic words. Syncategorematic words normally link object-words. But if the putative object-words in the sentence are not ostensively definable, the sentence is literally meaningless. In short, such empiricists would have us understand that if it is not possible to point to, or in some other way empirically indicate, what a non-syncategorematic word stands for, that word is meaningless.

It is because of this condition of meaningfulness that science and common-sense claims make sense while theology does not, for 'God' and 'nirvana' are plainly not syncategorematic and yet they are most certainly not ostensively definable. It is a category mistake to think they are, for

35

anyone who knows how properly to employ them knows that there cannot be any question of locating God or nirvana with a telescope, microscope or radar beam or with the unaided human senses. God — the maker of the world, the infinite individual transcendent to the world — is by definition not an observable reality. But this makes 'God' literally meaningless — what Ayer called a metaphysical word — and God an *ersatz* reality.

However, the counter is that the theory of meaning underlying this claim is radically mistaken. That is to say, the following thesis about meaning is in error: all words are either object-words or syncategorematic words, and the former are meaningful (genuine words) only if it is at least in principle possible ostensively to define them. As J. L. Evans points out in his 'The Foundations of Empiricism', to dichotomise words in this simple way 'represents a gross over-simplification of the types of words of which language is composed' (3). The category object-words 'will have to contain, e.g. proper names, prepositions, etc., in spite of the obvious logical differences in the ways in which they function' (4). The empiricist criterion of meaning is in reality unempirical, for while it is at least plausible to maintain that 'John', 'green', 'chair' must be ostensively definable if they are to have meaning, it is not only such perplexing and suspect terms as 'God', 'immortality' and 'nirvana' which are not ostensively definable, but also such unequivocally meaningful terms as 'that', 'he', 'spontaneity', 'was', 'merely', 'random', 'of' and the like. There is no pointing to what they mean as is the case with 'John' or even 'red'.

If we take the heroic course of sticking with such an empiricist criterion of meaning while restricting the category object-words 'to those words whose *referends* are directly observable, or to those words which stand for sensible things or properties of things, i.e to nouns like "table" or adjectives like "red" ', then we simply rule out as meaningless not merely metaphysical and theological words but everyday words integral to scientific and common-sense discourses. But this commits us to treating as meaningless words which no empiricist or anyone else in his right mind would wish to rule out as meaningless. Yet with the abandonment of the claim that all meaningful words are either syncategorematic words or object-words, we have lost our warrant for maintaining that a sentence is literally meaningless unless all its non-syncategorematic terms are ostensively definable. Moreover, it is not the case that a non-syncategorematic term is meaningful only if it is either ostensively definable or in turn verbally definable in terms of words which are ostensively definable. Such a claim is perhaps plausible for 'colour' or 'tone' or 'tribe' but hardly for 'that', 'spontaneity' or 'prosper' or such meaningful but utterly theoretical terms as 'electric field of force' or 'Schrödinger wave-function' which are indeed far from the experiential periphery and indeed get their meaning from the role they play in a scientific system. There is, in short, much more semantical stratification in language than the above empiricist account allows. Terms for theoretical concepts of such a high degree of abstractness are not and cannot be fully defined by reference to terms which are in turn ostensively definable.

The empiricist critics of religion would not dream of maintaining that these theoretical terms in science are not meaningful. But then why not allow that 'God' is also a meaningful term? It is a word expressive of an abstract concept deeply embedded in Jewish and Christian theological systems and indeed in Judaism and Christianity themselves. It gets its meaning from the role it plays in the Jewish and Christian forms of life. There are theoretical terms in physics which are not even indirectly ostensively definable but are plainly meaningful. Why be so discriminatory against theology? The situations seem at least to be quite parallel. To continue to maintain that 'God' is devoid of literal meaning and that a non-syncategorematic word is meaningful only if it is ostensively definable is to make a dogmatic and unwarranted conceptual restriction. If the theoretical terms of science are held to be meaningful, it is arbitrary to rule out God-talk, and if only those non-syncategorematic terms which are directly or indirectly ostensively definable are taken to be meaningful, a host of words that empiricist and non-empiricist alike regard as meaningful must be ruled out as meaningless. To remain committed to such an empiricist criterion is to be held captive by an arbitrary dogma.

Such arguments do establish that we should abandon the empiricist criterion that a non-syncategorematic word or term is literally meaningful only if it is ostensively definable, but there is still *Lebensraum* for the empiricist critic of religion. Indeed, not all non-syncategorematic terms function as object-words, but 'God', i.e. 'The Creator of the heavens and the earth' or 'The unique, uncreated, omnipotent and omniscient, infinite, personal, pure, eternal spirit who has created everything other than himself', 'The transcendent Supreme reality without limit' or 'He who laid the foundations of the earth' (Psalm 104), is surely clearly a putative object-word or a referring expression whether viewed as a name or as a definite description or some hybrid. And thus concerning 'God' it is clearly in order to ask how what it supposedly denotes or refers to is to be identified. It is not that 'God' means what it refers to — one should not collapse meaning and reference — but that as a putative referring expression we must know what it would be like for it to refer in order to understand what is meant by it. It indeed can refer in the absence of a referent, but for it to be a genuine referring expression, we must understand what would count as a referent of such a term. Otherwise we cannot understand what is asserted or denied when it is used. In fine, we must have some idea of what it would be like for 'God' actually to make reference or fail to make reference. But this is just our puzzlement. We seem to have no way of identifying the referent of 'God'. Since whatever it is, it is not something literally observable like a rock, a germ, a distant star or something we could become directly aware of like a pain or an anxiety, it is not clear what, if anything, is actually being referred to or could be referred to by 'God' given its present use in the language. The referent of 'God' cannot be something given in experience, but then how can we come to understand what is meant by it?

'God' is not ostensively teachable, but it is equally difficult to teach intralinguistically, for the putative descriptions used to specify what is meant by 'God' are as problematic as 'God'. That is, if we are puzzled by what 'God' supposedly refers to, we are going to be equally puzzled by 'the maker of the heavens and the earth', 'the uncaused creator of all finite reality', 'the sole absolutely unlimited being', 'the unconditioned transcendent', 'He Who is', 'the wholly other', 'the infinite individual' and the like. The putative referents for these terms remain as puzzling as the putative referent for 'God', and when we try to make assertions with grammatically well-formed sentences utilising such a theological and/or religious vocabulary, it becomes evident that we do not know how to make truth-claims utilising such sentences. 'The maker of the heavens and the earth created everything other than himself out of nothing', 'There is an infinite individual who is wholly good and loving' or 'There is a transcendent cause of the universe' are all without a determinate truth-value. And this seems at least to be a disaster for religion when we recall that to believe is to believe something. For this means it ought to be possible in some way to say what the difference is between what one believes to be true and what one believes not to be true, if indeed there is really anything intelligible that one believes and one is not just under an illusion that one believes. It is here, empiricist critics of religion argue, where we are stuck with non-anthropomorphic God-talk. And being stuck here has nothing to do with a commitment to phenomenalism, the priority of ostensive definitions or to some naive classificatory system that divides up all meaningful words into object-words and syncategorematic terms. Neither the believer nor the sceptic can give directions which would test (confirm or inform) the truth of what he allegedly claims in trying to use God-talk assertively. 'There is a transcendent creator of the world' and 'It is not the case that there is such a creator' both seem to be equally compatible with any actual or conceivable empirically identifiable turn of events or states of affairs. That is to say, there seems to be no experienceable difference, except in what goes on in the personality of the asserter or denier, between asserting there is such a transcendent cause and denying it. And what goes on in the personality of the maker of such putative factual claims can hardly be relevant to its truth. That I am heartened by the claim, saddened by the claim or indifferent to the claim does not affect its truth-value, if it is what it purports to be, namely an objective, non-psychological statement of fact. That is to say, facts about the pro-attitudes towards such statements have no tendency to show what it would be like for them to be true or false, let alone that they are true. For whatever it is

39

that we are allegedly asserting if we are making a genuine factual assertion, it must be possible to show what it would be like for the assertion to be true or probably true and what it would be like for the assertion to be false or probably false. If that condition does not obtain, if God-talk does not lay itself open to experiential confirmation or disconfirmation in this way (not conclusive verification or falsification), it, no matter how emotively meaningful, is without factual significance and makes no genuine truth-claim. This much in the empiricist critique seems at least to survive the dissolution of logical empiricism.

II

Even such a modified empiricist critique of religion has failed to staisfy many. It is now evident that it is a mistake to say that a grammatically and syntactically well-formed putative factual assertion is only a genuine factual assertion (a genuine material truth-claim) if it refers to objects which are given in sense-experience. 'Photon', for example, does not refer to something that is in fact given in sense-experience, and the theory in which this term is embedded is such that it is not to be expected that at some later date photons will become observable. But there is still an empirical specification of their meaning, for statements in which the term 'photon' is used are confirmable or infirmable. There is agreement on all sides about such considerations, but there remains the feeling that even a more modest empiricist critique of theology, which repudiates such radical empiricism, is still misdirected.

E. L. Mascall, for example, argues in 'Words and Images' that there are crushing difficulties in such verificationism; difficulties that allegedly remain even after the amendments and reduction of claims mentioned above have been made.

Mascall, like many others, has difficulty with the verifiability principle itself. Even if we only take it — as indeed it should be taken — as a criterion of factual significance, as a litmus-paper test for determining which of the various statements we make have factual significance and which factual-appearing statements are without such significance, we still have to ask about the status of the principle itself: 'A sentence is used to make a factual statement only if the

40

statement it makes is at least in principle confirmable or infirmable'. Is that statement itself verifiable (confirmable or infirmable)? Taken as an empirical hypothesis about language, it is indeed verifiable; but it most certainly appears at least on such a construal to be plainly false. There are many sentences which fluent speakers believe are factual statements but which they also believe are not verifiable. That is, many fluent speakers believe they are statements of fact but not verifiable (confirmable or infirmable) statements of fact. I think the issue here is more complex than would appear from the foregoing, but it is unnecessary to go into these alleged complexities, for defenders of the verifiability criterion do not want to take it as an empirical hypothesis, but, as Ayer puts it in 'Language, Truth and Logic', 'as a definition' and as a definition 'which is not supposed to be entirely arbitrary' (5). So the answer to our question should be that it is plainly not verifiable because it is analytic.

Mascall pounces on this and claims that Ayer is being evasive here. He thinks Ayer is trying to run with the hare and hunt with the hounds, for 'the assertion that the principle is a definition makes it impossible to question its truth, while the assertion that it is not entirely arbitrary suggests that some ground for its assertion is to be found in experience' (6). However, here it is Mascall who is confused. Reportive or lexical definitions, e.g. 'Puppies are young dogs', are clearly true or false, some are non-arbitrary (all good or plausible ones in fact) and their ground is to be found in experience, e.g. in the linguistic behaviour of the users of the language in question. But — and these are the kinds of definitions Ayer has in mind — persuasive or reforming definitions involving an element of stipulation are indeed neither true nor false, but are either useful or useless, reasonable or unreasonable, non-arbitrary or arbitrary, and whether they have these features is, within the limits of vagueness of the concepts in question, establishable by empirical investigation. If, for example, instead of defining a 'primitive culture' as a 'non-literate culture', a group of anthropologists said 'Always and only take a primitive culture to be a culture like a pre-literate Amazonian culture', their reforming definition could be easily shown to be useless (for most purposes), unreasonable and arbitrary.

41

However, if Ayer's defnition is to be other than arbitrary, it must be the case that in asserting that an unverifiable statement is factually meaningless he is not using 'factually' or 'meaningless' in a Pickwickian sense. But Mascall thinks he is being Pickwickian. Here Mascall has considerable support and here it is less evident where the confusion lies. He maintains that Ayer never establishes that unverifiable utterances are factually meaningless or unintelligible in any common or garden sense of these terms. Ayer is simply making, in Mascall's judgement, his own rather special stipulations. Others can with equal legitimacy make other stipulations and no good reasons have been given why we should accept those Ayer or Ayer-like stipulations which would put non-anthropomorphic God-talk out of business as a literal form of discourse. Ayer's definition, Mascall remarks, indeed records his own methodological principle, but he has given us no good grounds for adopting it. Rather, it seems to be merely expressive of his 'own preferences and habits'.

Ayer's remarks, Mascall continues, subsequent to the first edition of his iconoclastic 'Language, Truth and Logic' exhibit a 'very skilful rearguard action, in which Ayer rapidly oscillates between a number of positions, treating the verification principle at one moment as a definition, at another as a truth of logic and another as an empirical, verified generalisation' (7). But, Mascall maintains, this is radically inconsistent with his own central contention that there is an 'absolute distinction between truths of logic and statements of empirical fact' (8).

I have already indicated a crucial confusion in Mascall's argument which shows that there is no such inconsistency, but I want to go on briefly to indicate that Ayer gives us a coherent account of the status of the verifiability principle which makes it evident that it is neither a metaphysical principle nor — to understate the claim — an unreasonable methodological principle. Mascall concerns himself only with 'Language, Truth and Logic', but Ayer, in a number of brief subsequent statements about this problem, has made his position on this issue tolerably clear and indeed quite plausible (9). Ayer maintains that if we become clear about what it is to understand a matter of fact, we will come to adopt his methodological principle. Non-verifiable statements are not, whatever other kind of meaning or use they may have, intelligible statements of fact. Note that Mascall on his own wishes to link meaningfulness, intelligibility and understanding. He thinks it is analytically true 'that in order to know whether a statement has meaning you should see whether it is possible to understand it' (10). Ayer maintains that to understand a statement of fact you have to know what would in principle confirm it or infirm it. For religious beliefs to remain viable in a way which would keep them at all close to traditional Jewish and Christian expectations, their central theological claims must be construed as factual statements — as truth-claims about the nature of the universe — and thus, Ayer is maintaining, to understand them, we must know what would be the case if they were true or probably true. This is no more than a conceptual or, if you will, a grammatical remark about what understanding comes to in such contexts. And knowing what would be the case if they were true or probably true involves knowing what observations would confirm or infirm them and that 'in turn means being disposed to accept certain situations as warranting the acceptance or rejection' of such statements. The content of factual statements is fixed by the range of situations and experiences that would substantiate the statements in question (11). In short, as Ayer puts it at the end of his debate with Father Copleston:

I understand a statement of fact if I know what to look for on the supposition that it is true. And my knowing what to look for is itself a matter of my being able to interpret the statement as referring at least to some possible experience (12).

In reply to the charge that the principle of verifiability is an arbitrary, unverifiable dogma, Ayer replies:

The principle of verifiability is not itself a descriptive statement. Its status is that of a persuasive definition. I am persuaded by it, but why should you be? Can I prove it? Yes, on the basis of other definitions. I have, in fact, tried to show you how it can be derived from an analysis of understanding (13).

These definitions try to encapsulate what in science and

43

everyday life we mean by 'understand', 'intelligible', 'communicate', 'know', 'idea' and the like. Ayer points out that they can, of course, be rejected, but only at a price, for they give us a useful, checkable system of thought, so that we can test our claims and fix our beliefs in a reliable manner. Systems involving metaphysical statements (including, of course, God-talk) are systems which commit one to asserting the existence of what Copleston calls a 'metaphysical reality' by which he means 'a being which in principle, and not merely in fact, transcends the sphere of what can be sensibly experienced' (14). But such 'systems of thought', though they allegedly provide us with 'metaphysical statements' which are claimed to be 'ultimate explanations of fact', are in reality systems which do not provide us with explanations in the ordinary sense of 'explanations'; they are 'systems of thought' which fail to supply any rules for the use of their key explanations, nor do we have a criterion for deciding when such metaphysical statements are true or false. Sticking with the discourses of science and common sense, with their verifiable claims, we can understand and communicate, but by utilising such metaphysical systems objective inquiry, communication and a warrantable belief become impossible to attain. Thus we have very good reasons for eliminating metaphysics, including natural theology.

Perhaps in some way that is not evident to me these arguments are in some way mistaken. Perhaps the concepts of verification and understanding a matter of fact are not as closely linked as Ayer believes; even so, in arguing this way we have not inconsistently appealed to a metaphysical dogma of our own. The verification principle itself does not need verification, for it is a definition; and as a persuasive definition it can be useful or useless and arbitrary. And whether a given persuasive definition such as Ayer's of 'factual intelligibility' or 'having factual content' is useful is open to empirical test (15).

Adopting the recommendations that such empiricist critics of religion set out about what to regard as a literally meaningful statement of fact has the disadvantage that it tends to blind one to the interest such metaphysical and theological questions do have. But it has the merit of removing the temptation to think that somehow the claims

44

of religion unveil for us or confront us with a profounder, deeper understanding of life and give us a grasp of some more ultimate order of fact than would otherwise be available to us. We are freed from the need to think that somehow — in a way which remains utterly mysterious — the secularism that is often the result of secularisation must be a shallow view of life. The secularist must indeed accept as normative for coming to understand what man and nature are like, and for making sense of life, the kinds of claims about the world which can be made by scientific and common-sense statements; and he must also reject as illusory all non-verifiable religious 'truth-claims'. But with our enhanced understanding of 'understanding', we now see that such a secularism need not be at all a shallower view of life than a religious or metaphysical view and we are freed from trying to answer what appear at least to be utterly unanswerable questions (16).

III

We are not quite at the end of the line, for Mascall has a further objection which is relevant here. He like others takes Ayer to task for having an overly narrow conception of experience. Ayer, Mascall complains, 'having made the apparently innocent and plausible assertion that all meaningful assertions must have some reference to experience ... goes on to limit the meaning of experience in the narrowest and most arbitrary way to the experience of the bodily senses' (17). Ayer, as contemporary empiricists generally, has been quick to repudiate this suggestion. After all, it is not the task of a philosopher to decide what kinds of experience there are. That is itself an empirical question. As Ayer puts it in his debate with Father Copleston: 'Nor do I wish to restrict experience to sense experience' (18).

However, this typical empiricist disclaimer to the contrary notwithstanding, Mascall could argue that Ayer's analysis in effect proceeds as if the only intelligible forms of experience are the various kinds of sensory experience. And this is just what Mascall does in his discussion of Ayer's remarks about mystical experience. Ayer notes and discusses the argument that the mystic can readily claim that his mystical intuitions (mystical states of consciousness) do 'reveal truths to him, even though he cannot explain to others what these truths are; and that we who do not possess this faculty of intuition can have no ground for denying that it is a cognitive faculty' (19). We cannot justifiably do this because we cannot reasonably maintain *a priori* that there are no ways of discovering what is the case other than our own. The answer is 'that we set no limit to the number of ways in which one may come to formulate a true proposition' (20). So far so good, but then Ayer goes on to make the remark to which Mascall takes exception:

> We do not deny *a priori* that the mystic is able to discover truths by his own special methods. We wait to hear what are the propositions which embody his discoveries, in order to see whether they are verified or confuted by our *empirical* observations. But the mystic, so far from producing propositions which are empirically verified, is unable to produce any intelligible propositions at all. And therefore we say that his intuition has not revealed to him any facts. It is no use his saying that he has apprehended facts but is unable to express them. For we know that if he really had acquired any information he would be able to express it (21).

Mascall remarks that the prima facie plausibility of this claim turns on failing to note an ambiguity in Ayer's use of 'empirical'. First, in order not to rule out *a priori* the relevance of mystical experience, Ayer uses 'empirical' in a very broad sense. But then in the use of 'empirical' italicised in the above quotation, where he speaks of checking the mystics' putative truth-claims, he uses 'empirical' in what Mascall calls 'an extremely specialised sense in order to rule out all experience except that of sense phenomena' (22). But why hold, Mascall asks, that the only test for the truth of the mystics' putative truth-claims are 'our empirical (presumably here, sensory) observations' (23)? Why cannot the mystic respond that there are non-sensory but not personally idiosyncratic experiences which some of the hearers at least have and which logically speaking all can have, if they undergo the appropriate training and develop a purity of

46

heart, and that such experiences are the experiences which will verify his propostions? Only if we smuggle in some restrictive concept of 'empirical' do his utterances become unverifiable.

Ayer's remarks about this in 'Language, Truth and Logic' are indeed confusing if not confused. However, his remarks to Father Copleston in their debate in effect meet Mascall's objections:

Not do I wish to restrict experience to sense experience: I should not at all mind counting what might be called introspectible experiences, or feelings, mystical experiences, if you like. It would be true, then, that people who haven't had certain experiences won't understand propositions which refer to them; but that I don't mind either. I can quite well believe that you have experiences different from mine. Let us assume (which, after all, is an empirical assumption) that you have even a sense different from mine. I should be in the position of the blind man, and then I should admit that statements which are unintelligible to me might be meaningful for you. But I should then go on to say that the factual content of yours *was* determined by the experiences which counted as their verifiers or falsifiers. (24)

If in asserting that he is directly aware of God someone means no more than that he is having a certain kind of experience, then indeed, as Ayer puts it in 'Language, Truth and Logic', the man's assertion may be true. But the man — Ayer should gave said the Jew, the Christian or the Moslem — who has such experiences ordinarily believes that he is directly aware of a transcendent being. But it is here, Ayer continues, where we have our difficulties, for, mystical experiences or not, 'There exists a transcendent God' has no factual or literal significance.

While surely there is nothing inconsistent or even conceptually odd or unhappy in affirming that there are states of mystical consciousness while denying that there is a God or any transcendent realities, it remains the case, Mascall argues, that Ayer's arguments here are question-begging and arbitrary.

47

The forms of language in the demanding modes of life which constitute mysticism are undoubtedly odd, paradoxical, and the 'way in which its language is related to the reality with which it is concerned . . . is indirect', but none the less it can be learned and, Mascall avers, understood. For him, this means that 'mystical experience in the strict sense' is taken to be 'a direct experimental awareness of God' (25). And what God tells us in such an encounter happens to be true, Mascall claims, and, he gives us to understand, Ayer is simply being arbitrary when he rules out by linguistic fiat 'that finite minds can apprehend a transcendent and infinite reality and that human language can communicate information about it . . . ' (26).

Mascall, note, does not even accept Ayer's weakened criterion for factual significance, i.e. a proposition has factual significance only if some observations, actual or possible, are relevant to the determination of its truth or falsity. For Mascall maintains that the mystic's specifically religious utterances are not verifiable or confutable by empirical observation, but all the same they are intelligible to those who will take the trouble to try to understand them. To deny that this is so, he tells us, 'is to make a dogma into a wall which hides the most obvious facts' (27).

However, what in this context does or does not hide the most obvious facts is not at all evident. But what is evident is (a) that both Ayer and Mascall give a very inadequate account of mystical experience, and (b) that we will be in a far better position to appraise Ayer's central claim that an appeal to mystical experience does not enable us to surmount the difficulties he finds in God-talk, once what we are talking about in speaking of mystical experience is made more precise.

First, it is well established that mystical experience is no illusion, if by that we mean that there occur for certain people identifiable and indeed describable states of consciousness which are properly called 'mystical states of consciousness'. It is also true that every form of consciousness is a consciousness of something — a grammatical remark about 'consciousness' — but it does not follow from this that mystical consciousness is about what mystics think it is about. (Indeed, they do not all think it is about the same thing. But even if they all agree, they could all be mistaken in their judgements as to what it is about.) Though this distinction in such a context is not a sharp one, we must distinguish between the experience itself and the interpretation of it. W. T. Stace and Ninian Smart are good guides here, and I shall follow them (28).

There is a reasonably determinate cluster of empirically identifiable features common to and distinctive of the various experiences which in the religions of the world are called 'mystical experiences'. They constitute the common core of mystical consciousness. There are — accommodatable within this common core — two types of mysticism, extravertive and introvertive. In both cases there is the consciousness of an indifferentiated unity. In the first case, it is felt to be an exterior reality with which one is in an intimate and striking rapport; in the second case, it is a state one finds by plumbing the depths of one's soul. Historically at least, introvertive mysticism has been the most important. In neither case is mystical consciousness the having of a literal vision, the hearing of voices, the feeling of awe or dependence or any other kind of feeling or the having of a sensation. It is, rather, said to be a non-sensory awareness or consciousness giving one, in its extravertive form, a unified comprehension of reality which is naturally expressed in the saying 'All things are one' or, in the introvertive form, an interior unitary consciousness resulting from an inner quest which is not characterisable in terms of mental images and the like. (The experience of *satori* is paradigmatic of such an introvertive mystical experience.)

The unifying consciousness that 'All is one' of the extravertive form is an awareness of 'the One' in and through the multiplicity of objects, and with that there is an awareness of the living presense of all things: 'Nothing is really dead.' Such a unitary reality as is experienced is taken to be *in some sense* ineffable though still absolutely real. Moreover, such a mystical consciousness carries with it a feeling of blessedness, joy and a sense of the sacred and the holy.

Introvertive forms of mystical experience have all the latter features, but instead of a unifying consciousness of the oneness of all things, there is a unifying consciousness from

49

which all the multiplicity of conceptual, sensuous or other empirical content has been excluded, so that there remains only a void or empty unity. And instead of a consciousness of the living presence of all things, there arises an idea of something essentially non-temporal, non-spatial and otherwise uninvolved. In both cases we have what is said to be a non-sensory awareness of an undifferentiated unity felt to be paradoxical, sacred, blessed, and *in some sense* ineffable.

In talking about mystical experience, it is extremely important, as I have already remarked, to distinguish, on the one hand, the experience itself and the description of that experience from, on the other hand, the interpretation of the experience. And do not say 'All descriptions are interpretations', for neither term could have a meaning if they were not distinguishable. What is reasonable behind the move to collapse the distinction between description and interpretation is the realisation that what here are called 'the same experiences' can be described in many different ways, and that for human actions and the like — presumably including mystical experiences — there are no brute descriptions reflecting some discoverable 'hard facts' which could rightly be said to be the only correct and irreducible description of what transpires (29).

The above accounts of extravertive and introvertive mystical experiences are intended as descriptions, close to the phenomenological core and not theory-laden. Compared to what is often said, it is indeed the case that they are not theory-laden, or at least as theory-laden as the usual theologically ramified accounts, and they appear at least to be doctrinally neutral. But there remain concepts in these descriptions which to me are perplexing, and though I am no student of mysticism and do not claim to be able to form phenomenologically purer descriptions which would still do justice to those experiences, it is not at all evident to me that purer and perhaps phenomenologically more adequate descriptions than the above could not in fact be given. But, be that as it may, these descriptions are comparatively brute when compared with Mascall's utterly ethnocentric and theologically developed characterisation of mystical experience in what he calls 'the strict sense' as 'a direct experimental awareness of God in which the senses play no

50

part'.

There is a conceptual distinction between description and interpretation even though a sharp line between the two cannot be drawn. And, vis-à-vis mystical experience, we have paradigms of each. The above characterisations of introvertive and extravertive mystical experiences are paradigmatic descriptions and the following are paradigms of interpretations:

(a) that in mystical experience one is united with Christ, or (b) that in mystical consciousness one attains the peace and insight of nirvana such that one will no longer be reborn, or (c) that mystical consciousness is a liberation in which the soul attains an isolation so that it is no longer implicated in nature and the round of rebirth, but is one with — that is, united with — an infinite number of eternal selves, or (d) that mystical consciousness is only an esoteric and striking rapport with nature and/or a sense of wholeness such that for a time one's attitudes towards life are fundamentally transformed.

Typically, interpretations made either by the person having the mystical experience or some other religious person are made in accordance with the religious traditions and with the theological doctrines of these traditions. Stace and Smart, by contrast, give a description of mystical experience which is doctrinally neutral. (There can be, of course, secularist as well as doctrinally inspired interpretations of mystical experience, e.g. Freud's talk of oceanic feelings. The important thing to see here is that both are distinct from these doctrinally neutral descriptions of mystical experience.)

Smart shows convincingly that introvertive mystical experiences of both monistic mysticism (Advatia, Sainkhya-Yoga, and the like) and the theistic mysticism of the Judaeo-Christian tradition and the Gita are the same and that there is even a good case for treating the mystical experience of the Theravadin as also being of the same mould. But while the experience is the same or for the most part the same, the interpretations of this common experience differ, and differ along doctrinal lines. That is to say, the adherents of these religions will typically give interpretations of their own experiences and of the experiences of others which are expanded in terms of their own doctrinal commitments.

51

A Christian, for example, recognises the Hindu mystic's mystical experience as the same as his own. But given the Christian's conception of God and worship, the Christian will say that it is a mistake to maintain that there is an identity between the experiencer and what is experienced, though he may well admit that with some risk one can speak of an identity here as a hyperbole used to bring out the dazzling and compelling quality of the encounter, but, he will insist, there is no literal identity between the experience and the ultimate reality experienced. There can be no such union. But a Hindu without such theistic doctrinal commitments can more happily interpret the experience as a union with an ultimate reality, and a Theravadian can dispense altogether with the concept of such an Absolute Reality. Nirvana is, after all, not a transcendent entity or substantial reality. The point is that one's interpretations (where one has mystical illumination) can conflict and the test of the correctness of the interpretation is not in terms of the mystical experience, which is the same, but must itself be made in accordance with one's evaluation of the relevant religious doctrines. A man, as Smart puts it, could have 'a genuine mystical experience, but be wrong in not according it to God's grace' (30). Or again, he might be right in not ascribing it to God's grace. A completely secular interpretation which invoked no conceptions of transcendent realities or states might, instead, be the correct interpretation. The point is that the mystical experience itself is religiously and theologically neutral, and careful phenomenological descriptions of the common core of mystical experience make this evident. The taking of such experience utterly seriously does not even commit one to 'the neo-Vedantin thesis that behind the various forms of religion there is a higher truth realizable in contemplative experience and best expressed through the dotrine of a universal Self (or Atman)', for the various and conflicting theological doctrines are equally compatible with the above core — theologically unramified — descriptions of the same mystical experience (31). The neo-Vedantian claim here is just as much an interpretation of experience as are the *other doctrinally ramified* characterisations. Therefore it cannot justly claim simply to be describing the relevant brute facts.

52

The central point to understand is that the truth of the interpretation of the mystical experience cannot be read off from the experience itself. Whether any of these theological doctrines used to interpret mystical experience are ever to be shown to be true or false will depend on evidence other than that which we gain through mystical experience. There is a widespread belief that certain individuals have gained religious knowledge or insight into the Transcendent through mystical experience, but whether this is so or not cannot be established by attending to mystical experience itself.

The application of these remarks about mystical experience to Mascall's criticism of Ayer is this. Mascall confuses a highly ethnocentric, doctrinally ramified and theologically biased interpretation of mystical experience with a description of mystical experience. His account would simply rule out as non-genuine the mystical experiences of Jainist, Theravadian and Taoist mystics. That is surely a *reductio* of such an interpretation. Moreover, even for Judaeo-Christian mystical experience, such an interpretation as Mascall's is not determined by the experience itself. He has not stuck to giving a description of what has been experienced but has passed off, as such a description, a highly ramified and theologically controversial interpretation of that experience. Ayer could readily grant (as indeed he should) that there are genuine mystical experiences while consistently denying that these experiences are a 'direct experimental or experiential awareness of God in which the senses play no part' or that the mystic gains a knowledge of 'a transcendent and infinite reality'.

Indeed, Mascall is right, the mystics do have their own way of talking, but the mystics come from radically different traditions and sometimes, though rarely, from no religious traditions at all, and these traditions conflict. The supposed reality allegedly apprehended by the mystic is, depending on the culture from which he comes, characterised in very different ways, and the manner in which it is characterised is largely a function of his own religious and theological tradition. When we stick to a sufficiently pure description of his experience to catch what is· common to the various mystics — to catch what makes it mystical experience — we have something that remains neutral with respect to all these theological and religious truth-claims. In going to the phenomenological heart of the matter, we come up with something that could be accepted as genuine by someone such as Ayer who regards talk of 'a transcendent and infinite reality' or 'a direct awareness of God' or even of the very concepts God, Atman or nirvana as devoid of literal significance. Ayer can perfectly well accommodate mystical experiences; his empirical base is not too narrow or his conception of experience too rigid. Mascall has not shown that Ayer has made any arbitrary moves at all.

In short, it may be the case that certain theological and religious propositions are unverifiable and still have factual significance and/or still make substantive truth-claims. It may be true that finite minds, as Mascall says, 'can apprehend a transcendent and infinite reality'. But Ayer and other empiricists have given us good reasons for thinking such claims are mistaken, and Mascall has done nothing to unsettle this empiricist challenge.

4 Rebuttals and Responses: II

The counter-reformation so far discussed against empiricist critiques of religion has come largely from outside of analytical philosophy, but there is also keen criticism from within which maintains that these empiricist critiques do not apply the analytic method thoroughly and rigorously enough but rely on too many vague claims and blur too many distinctions. A rigorous application of conceptual analysis will show that such empiricist critiques are themselves really at best unsupported dogmas and at worst incoherent claims (1). These are strong and important contentions. I shall consider them by examining the arguments of their best adversaries.

One way — as we have seen — of forcefully stating the empiricist challenge concerning the literal intelligibility of such religious and theological utterances as 'Jesus is the son of God' and 'God loves mankind' is to raise questions about their falsifiability. If they are in principle utterly un-falsifiable, they — to put the matter crudely — are devoid of factual significance. The challenge in question has been dubbed Flew's challenge.

In his 'God and Other Minds', Alvin Plantinga asks: 'How are we to understand Flew's challenge? What exactly is he requiring of theological statements? Is he chiding the theist for ignoring some version of the verifiability criterion? If so, which version?' (2). With any of the standard versions, Plantinga maintains, Flew would be in trouble, for 'no one has succeeded in stating a version of the verifiability criterion that is even remotely plausible . . . ' (3). Flew's challenge, he continues, has not been stated by Flew or by anyone else with sufficient intelligibility for us to be able even to determine what the challenge is, let alone to determine its legitimacy (4). From this, Plantinga concludes that those theologians who have taken this challenge seriously have been taken in by philosophers. Plantinga would have us believe that it poses no serious challenge to theology, for 'as a piece of natural atheology, verificationism is entirely unsuccessful' (5).

Plantinga states his case with rigour and economy. Many, I suspect, will believe he has said the last word on the subject. Since I am convinced that verificationism poses a fundamental problem for theology, it behoves me to begin this chapter by examining Plantinga's effort to dispose of this particular bit of atheology.

I shall commence with a statement of what I take to be the proper way of formulating Flew's challenge. Presupposed in such a challenge is the belief that there are central putative truth-claims in the Jewish-Christian tradition, such as the claim that God governs the world, which at least purport to be factual claims, and that if they are not genuinely factual claims, Jewish and Christian belief would be something radically different from what it is believed by the faithful to be (6). That is to say, within the mainstream of Judaism and Christianity, such utterances as 'God governs the world' are believed to be assertions, true or false. Moreover, it is also believed by the faithful that their being assertions and indeed being true is a fact which is of fundamental importance for the destiny of mankind. This means — and Plantinga of course does not deny this — that putative assertions such as 'God governs the world' must deny many other assertions and exclude many states of affairs. Flew's challenge stresses this, but it makes a stronger claim as well without which it would not be a challenge at all.

What is this stronger claim? It claims that if such putative factual assertions as 'God governs the world' are genuine factual assertions, they must exclude some conceivable happening, event or empirically identifiable process or state. Flew is maintaining, and I have maintained as well, that if a religious assertion is a bona fide factual assertion, it must at least be logically possible to specify in non-religious, non-theological terms what conceivable evidence would count against its truth (7). Religious propositions purporting to make factual assertions must at least be confirmable or infirmable in principle by non-religious, straightforwardly empirical, factual statements. The operative principle here is that a statement would never unequivocally count as a factual statement unless it were at least in principle confirmable or infirmable, i.e. unless at least some conceivable, empirically determinable state of affairs would count against its truth and some at least conceivable, empirically determinable state of affairs would count for its truth. Flew's challenge is just this: Believers take their central religious affirmations to be factual truth-claims, but if they actually are such truth-claims, it must be possible (logically possible) with respect to any religious truth-claim, on the one hand, to describe two empirically identifiable but distinct situations or states, one of which actually obtains when the religious statement in question is true, the other when it is false or, on the other hand and less determinately, at least if one situation or state obtains, we will have good grounds for saying the religious statement in question is true, and if the other obtains, we have good grounds for saying that it is false. If it is impossible even to conceive of any such conditions, then the putatively factual religious statement is neither true nor false. And thus it is not a factual statement at all. Flew's challenge is a challenge to the believer to state these conditions of confirmation or infirmation for their central theistic claims, e.g. 'God governs the world', 'God loves mankind' and 'There is a God'.

I have thus answered Plantinga's question about what the challenge is and what it requires of religious statements. Now I must turn to a consideration of Plantinga's claim that such a challenge is without merit and poses no legitimate threat for the believer or theologian. Part of what I take to be Plantinga's confusion results from his failure to recognise and correctly identify the challenge. Having failed to do this, he thinks that by showing the inadequacies of certain formulations of the verifiability criterion of meaning, he can establish the untenability of Flew's challenge.

In making the challenge, as I have made it, one is not maintaining, as Plantinga believes, that 'meaningful assertions must be falsifiable by some *empirical* state of affairs or some proposition with *empirical* content', but that if a meaningful sentence (a pleonasm) is used to make a factual statement that this statement, in order to be a genuine factual statement, must be in principle confirmable or infirmable by some proposition or set of propositions with empirical content (8). That is to say, a putatively factual statement actually has factual significance (is factually meaningful, has factual content) only if some differential experience is relevant to its truth or falsity. Moreover, it is simply gratuitous to assume, as Plantinga does, that if a statement is factual, there must be some finite and consistent set of observation statements which entail its denial, if it is verifiable or falsifiable or — as I would prefer to put it — confirmable or infirmable. We should have learned enough about the function of natural languages by now not to be always in search of that analytic ideal (9). It is enough that we can conceive of some observation statements which count for its truth and some against it.

Plantinga, however, might accept the modification that it is a criterion of factual significance or a principle of demarcation between statements which have genuine factual import and those that do not, and still maintain that such a criterion fails as a criterion of factual significance. To urge, that is, a criterion of factual significance is to maintain that, for any given natural language, statements are made when and only when sentences in that language are employed to make statements which are at least in principle empirically confirmable or infirmable. In other words, the criterion for whether a statement is a factual statement is whether it is so confirmable or infirmable. Plantinga presumably would still want to maintain that such a criterion, depending exactly on how it is taken, is either so restrictive that it excludes some paradigms of factual statements which verificationists would themselves unhesitatingly take to be factual statements or so liberal as to exclude no statements at all (10). I agree with Plantinga that if this were a consequence of adopting the criterion, it would be an inadequate criterion indeed. But it seems to me that this is not a consequence of the verificationist appeal in Flew's challenge as I have stated it.

Let us first consider if it is too restrictive. If the criterion of factual significance (factual import) is such that a statement to have such significance must be in principle decisively falsifiable, then 'There is at least one pink unicorn' or any other such existential statement is devoid of factual significance, but utterances of this type plainly have empirical import and thus they have factual significance.

However, the challenge as I have formulated it says nothing about such decisive falsifiability (11). It speaks of confirmability or infirmability: some experiential events, processes or states, if they were to occur or obtain, must count for or against the truth of a factual statement. That is, something which is differentially experienceable must be relevant to its truth or falsity. And put in this way, it also does not rule out universal statements such as 'All crows are black', for, while nothing would decisively confirm this statement, there is much evidence for its truth and thus it is plainly confirmable as well as infirmable. Nor need it rule out statements of mixed quantification such as 'Every human being has some neurotic traits', 'Every democracy has some Fascists', or 'Every culture has some people with naturally green hair' as being devoid of factual content. There are, as Carnap and Hempel have shown, no finite and consistent sets of statements which entail either the truth or the falsity of such statements. In that sense they are equally compatible with all conceivable experienceable happenings. But this is not to say that they are not confirmable or infirmable, for plainly some things count for or against their truth or falsity. Consider 'Every culture has some people with naturally green hair'. That we have carefully examined different cultures and different races at different times and never found anyone with green hair surely counts, though not at all decisively, against the truth of such a statement. Moreover, the independently confirmable and infirmable statements of biological theory count against its truth as well. What is true is what with statements of mixed quantification the very notion of even in principle decisive confirmation of disconfirmation is unexemplifiable. Such statements are unfalsifiable in the sense that there are no finite and consistent sets of observation statements that entail their denial and none that entail their affirmation. But so what? We are not requiring such a decisive confirmation or disconfirmation and we are not making the gratuitous assumption that there must be some finite and consistent sets of observation statements which would entail, depending on what they are, either the affirmation or denial of any genuine factual statement. Such a rationalist stress on entailment seems entirely out of place. Rather, I am only stressing, as Ayer has come to, that a statement is a factual statement only if some kind of observation is relevant to its truth or falsity (12).

I am maintaining that only if some at least in principle observable state of affairs or happenings or series of happenings counts against its truth and some at least in principle observable state of affairs or happenings or series of happenings counts for its truth, can a statement properly be called a factual statement. None of the counter-examples offered by Plantinga or the traditional counter-examples — including statements of mixed quantification — fail to have factual content on this criterion. I challenge Plantinga or anyone else to provide a single counter-example of a statement not so confirmable or infirmable which is un-equivocally taken to be a factual statement by a fair sample of native or fluent speakers of the language in which the statement is expressed. (This is not pulling oneself up by one's own bootstraps, for if it were not possible for native speakers to recognise clear cases of factual and non-factual discourse, e.g. 'The butter is on the table' and 'Pass the butter', independently of *stating* or *recognising* a criterion, there would be no possibility of arguing about a criterion of factual significance.) No such counter-examples have been produced and the criterion does square with what in practice we take without hesitation to be factual statements and it provides us with a rationale for settling problematic cases. So it seems evident that Plantinga has not established that the criterion implicit in Flew's challenge is too restrictive.

However, Plantinga might more plausibly argue that, as I have stated it, the verifiability principle becomes too liberal since it lets in many, questionable metaphysical statements as well as religious statements such as 'God governs the world'. That is, contrary to my claim, it does not after all provide us with a criterion for settling problematic cases. Riots, plagues, loss of faith, wars, are taken by some to count against the claim that God governs the world; human love, a sense of the numinous, concern for social justice, and a commitment to human solidarity are taken by some to count for it. And at least some of these are plainly empirical conditions.

It is evident enough — and I have stressed this and so has Flew — that there are some employments of 'God governs the world' and the like where it does function as a meaningful

60

empirical statement quite open to confirmation or disconfirmation. There is nothing in Flew's challenge to rule out
such anthropomorphic conceptions of deity as being without
factual significance. Their actual specific factual significance
gives us good grounds for thinking that such religious claims
are false, and furthermore, D. Z. Phillips seems to me on solid
ground when he claims that such a concept of God would
also be religiously inappropriate (13). There is, however, a
strong tendency among the sophisticated faithful to treat
religious claims in such a way that they are not even in our
weak sense confirmable or infirmable. It is customary for
such believers to maintain that there is no experience or set
of experiences, either from without or from within, that
could possibly destroy religious faith. The central claims of
Christianity, for example, are taken to be completely
immune to disconfirmation by anything we could learn from
science or history or by any conceivable empirical observation or rational argument. The central doctrinal claims of
Christianity are thought to be factual assertions, but factual
assertions of a unique sort. They are the fundamental
absolute presuppositions of the faith. They underlie the
possibility of empirical test for more specific factual
assertions, but they are not themselves even in principle
confirmable or infirmable. When this turn is taken, as it is so
frequently in religious circles, then Flew's challenge becomes
relevant, for the key religious utterances of such people, while
remaining putatively factual, have actually ceased to make
any factual claim at all. At least so it seems, and so indeed it
would be if the criterion of factual significance implicit in my
statement of Flew's challenge is correct. Remember it does
not assert that 'God governs the world' and the like are
without factual significance, but that they are without
factual significance *if* they are not so confirmable or
infirmable.

It would seem to me that what Plantinga should say here in
defence of theism is this: Anthropomorphism is indeed a
mistake. No religious truth is to be discovered given such
thinking, but in flying from anthropomorphism, one must
not fall into the trap of claiming that the central claims of
one's religion are completely immune to confirmation or
infirmation or to any kind of empirical test. Such immunity

would indeed make them die the death of a thousand qualifications. We recognise that they, even when construed in a non-anthropomorphic way, are weakly confirmable and infirmable, though, as appropriate to such mysterious general cosmological claims, nothing even approaching decisiveness could possibly obtain here. But something does count in a weak but definitely empirical manner against them as well as for them. As men of faith, we with passionate inwardness commit ourselves to the view that they are true. We do not, and indeed cannot, know they are true; rather, we accept it as an unswerving article of faith that they are true. The certainty is not in the statement 'God governs the world', for it is a contingent empirical statement whose truth or falsity can never be infallibly determined, but in our commitment, i.e. in our determination to believe that it is true even if evidence to the contrary is very strong. Moreover, given the generality of such religious claims, a request for decisive confirmation or infirmation is entirely out of place. It is not reasonable to ask us to withhold assent until we can know or have good grounds for believing they are true, for concerning claims of such generality we can never be in a position to make such a test and thus be in a position to claim knowledge or justified belief. Here we must live by faith. And given the fact that this faith answers deep human needs and, if it is a true account of things, answers to still other distinctive human needs not otherwise satisfiable, it is not at all irrational but indeed quite reasonable to live by faith alone even though we have not the slightest reason to believe that our putative religious truth-claims are true (14).

Perhaps such a theist is after all being irrational, but irrational or not, if he takes that approach, it is natural to respond, he has appropriately enough met Flew's challenge head-on. I am somewhat ambivalent here about what to say, but it seems to me what should be said is this: The answer should be 'Yes' *and* 'No'. On the one hand, he has met it head on in the sense that he has pointed to the type of empirical conditions which he takes as counting for and against his basic religious claims and he has shown that, given what these claims are, it is inappropriate to ask for decisive or conclusive evidence for the truth or falsity of his putative truth-claims. After all, the object of our discourse here is supposed to be a mystery. In this way, the answer should be 'Yes'. On the other hand, the answer should be 'No', if it is thought that it has been established that 'God governs the world' and the like have factual significance on the criteria we have given. If 'God governs the world' did have such significance, it would have to have a different empirical content than does 'It is not the case that God governs the world' or 'God does not govern the world'. Recall that there must at least be some conceivable experience which is relevant to its truth or falsity. But this is not the case for 'God governs the world' and the like (15). Note that the non-believer might very well accept the believer's claims about human love, a sense of the numinous, a concern for social justice, and the incidence of commitments to human solidarity and still not at all see how this gives us grounds for believing in God or even gives an empirical anchorage to God-talk. He could ask if 'God' is just a compendious umbrella term for empirical phenomena of the sort just alluded to — a convenient theoretical device to use in talking of such matters, for it links many things together. But the theist would have to deny that it had only that meaning. After all, we are trying to talk about what is called 'a transcendent reality', 'an infinite world-ground', 'the source of all finite beings', 'an absolutely independent reality' or 'an infinite non-spatial temporal individual'. But such a non-believer might find talk of an infinite self-existent creator of all things other than Himself quite incomprehensible. The believer has pointed to some phenomena which allegedly confirms his claim 'God governs the world', but the non-believer asserts that it is not the case that God governs the world. They both agree about the relevant happenings in the world and now — since the believer steadfastly maintains that he is 'not just talking about what happens in the world' — the non-believer challenges him to say what is the empirical difference between the putative factual statement 'God governs the world' and 'It is not the case that God governs the world'? Both statements (given a sophisticated believer's use) seem equally compatible with all actual and conceivable empirical phenomena — including, of course, the empirical phenomena which the believer indicates as counting as evidence for his claim. If this is so, are they not both, since one is presumably the contradictory of the other, devoid of factual content? Remember, as we have learned from Duhem and Quine, we should not take statements in isolation when considering their confirmability and infirmability. 'God governs the world' — in non-anthropomorphic God-talk — seems at least to belong to a system of statements in which it is impossible to distinguish an empirical content which is different from that of its contradictory.

It is not that I am asking for decisiveness here, but simply for some empirical evidence which will count for the truth of the one putative truth-claim and against the other, so that they are *empirically* and not just *verbally* distinct utterances. But it is just this which the non-anthropomorphite seems at least incapable of providing for statements such as 'God governs the world' and 'It is not the case that God governs the world'. And this seems generally to obtain for fundamental putative religious truth-claims. Since this is so, there is a very strong sense in which Flew's challenge remains in force: The believer must in principle at least be able to show what empirical states of affairs (what differential experience) would count as evidence for his statement that would not be equally compatible with the contradictory of his statement. Unless he can do that, we in a very important sense do not know what would count as evidence for his claim, or against it, for it is empirically indistinguishable, as far as its alleged truth-value goes, from its contradictory. But this condition seems at least to obtain for non-anthropomorphites.

It will not do to reply that a non-believer who found the concept of God incomprehensible could not contradict 'God governs the world' because he would not understand it. When it is said that 'It is not the case that God governs the world', a number of things could be meant besides 'We know there is no God' or 'We have good grounds for believing that nothing governs the world'. One thing that could be meant is this: 'The concept of God is so incoherent or so indeterminate that one could not be justified in making such putative assertions as "God governs the world".'

Thus, if what I have argued here is substantially correct, there is an important sense in which Flew's challenge — that is, a fundamental empiricist challenge — remains unanswered

64

and very much needs to be answered by the theologian.

II

However, Plantinga might withdraw to his second line of defence. That is to say, even if such a criterion of factual significance can be stated in such a way that it is neither too restrictive nor too liberal, the question still remains: Why accept it? Why could not the theist respond as follows: Your criterion is plainly mistaken. Many statements made by theologians or plain religious people are neither analytic nor empirically verifiable (confirmable or infirmable). But they are still true or false statements which we understand and use in making assertions about our world. Thus it is false that only verifiable statements have factual significance.

With either an assumed or genuine historical naiveté which ignores the literature, Plantinga asks 'What could the verificationist reply? What sort of argument could he bring forward to show the theologian that he ought to accept the verifiability criterion and stop proclaiming these meaningless theological pseudo-statements?' (16). Ignoring what has been said in reply, Plantinga remarks that about all the verificationist 'could say here would be that his criterion does fit scientific and common-sense statements and does not fit theological statements' (17). From there on, Plantinga, of course, has an easy time of it, for it is perfectly true that if the empiricist critic of theism made such a weak defence, the theologian could quite properly respond: ' . . . there are, no doubt, many properties which distinguish scientific and common-sense statements from theological statements. But, of course, that does not suffice to show that theological statements are meaningless or logically out of order or anything of the sort' (18).

Fortunately for such empiricist critics of religion, there is a far stronger line of reply open to verificationists. One such reply is given a summary statement by A. J. Ayer at the end of his debate with Father Copleston (19). Theological statements such as 'God loves mankind', 'God governs the world' or even 'There is a God' are putative statements of fact. The faithful *believe* that they are true substantive statements; that is, they believe that they assert something that is so and that this something is extremely important. (That they believe it is so does not, of course, make it so. We must not confuse our *beliefs about* the discourse with the discourse.) But what is it, Ayer asks, to *understand* a statement of fact? He replies that to understand a statement of fact is to know 'what to look for on the supposition that it is true' (20). Furthermore, 'knowing what to look for is itself a matter of ... being able to interpret the statement as referring at least to some possible experience'. But why accept this, it may in turn be asked, why insist that this is the only way to understand a statement of fact? Ayer thinks that such a criterion can be justified if we consider with care what it is to get clear about what constitutes an understanding of something. Consider the kind of theological and/or metaphysical statements that theologians put forth as true or false, ultimate explanations of fact or assertions of some allegedly ultimate order of fact, e.g. 'God governs the world'. Some people say they understand such statements and no doubt sincerely believe they understand them, but they have no way of deciding (even tentatively) whether they are true or false or even probably true or false. They do not even understand what it would be like to set out to do this for such statements. They are as lost with such theological propositions as they would be with 'It is nightfall on the sun'. But in such a circumstance, what could it mean to claim to understand something? No sense has been given to the utterance that we understand something to be the case and yet we have no idea even of what could count towards deciding whether it is true or false.

One need not, of course, have an actual decision procedure for deciding whether the statement in question is true or false in order to understand it. We only must (or so it would seem) have some idea of what would count for or against its truth. To see this, Ayer claims, is to see how 'understand' functions in our actual discourse; that is, it is to see how, where the language is plainly not idling, we, as native or fluent speakers, would exhibit by our actual linguistic practices that it would be proper to say that we understand something. Note that if someone uttered 'It is nightfall on the sun', 'Wallace sleeps slower than Nixon', 'Colours speak faster than the speed of

66

light', 'There is a time-machine in Karlsruhe', or 'Physics is more mobile than chemistry', we would not understand these utterances until we had some idea of what it would be like for them to be true or false. As Coburn points out, such utterances have a certain pictorial meaning for us, but that does not at all mean that they can be used to make true or false statements or that we understand them as truth-claims (21).

Ayer gets us to ask, what would it be like to have some idea of what must obtain for a statement of fact to be true or false? It would be to know, he answers, what kind of experiences we would have if the statement were true or probably true and what kind of experiences we would have if it were false or probably false.

If Plantinga were to reply that this criterion is too narrow since it applies only to common-sense and scientific statements of fact, I would in turn challenge him to provide one example of an utterence that would quite unequivocally be generally accepted as an example of an utterance that would quite unequivocally be generally accepted as a statement of fact that is not so confirmable or infirmable. If he cannot — and I do not think he can — and no one else can either then we have reasonalbe grounds for believing that it is the case that, given our employments of 'fact', 'true', 'understand', 'statement of fact' and the like, we should say that 'God governs the world' is only a putative factual statement — a statement with pictorial meaning but without factual significance. It purports to make a theological truth-claim of capital importance, but actually fails to make such a claim, and the same thing holds for other fundamental theistic utterances. The conditions essential for understanding them are absent. No matter how much we may want to accept them on faith, we cannot, for we do not know *what* it is we are to believe to accept them on faith (22).

Plantinga could reply (as Alston has) that such an empiricist rebuttal conflates matters that should be kept distinct (23). It is a truism to say that a statement has assertive force only if there is some way, empirical or otherwise, of indicating that what one asserts is true or false or is probably true or false. One cannot admit that one understands a statement of fact and deny that this relation holds. But it is something else again to claim that the detecting must be empirical or experiential. How can one (or can one) establish Ayer's claim that to understand an assertion, claiming to be a matter of fact, one must have some conception of what would constitute at least a weak empirical or experiential test for it?

Consider 'Every property inheres in a substratum', 'Energy is everywhere and eternal', 'Properties exist apart from their exemplifications', 'Nothing exists but particulars', or 'God acts in the world'. Suppose it is asserted that they can be known to be true or false by a non-sensory intellectual intuition, though they are unverifiable in principle. If one has the proper intuition, one understands them; if not, not. Such statements are not meant to be statements about particular matters of fact. They are neither predictions nor retrodictions. They are about *all* of reality and they thus are not verifiable as are ordinary statements of fact. But for all that they are not meaningless or devoid of factual intelligibility. Yet when one reflects on the very meaning of such utterances one can readily see that they could not be empirically verifiable. What, then, is the justification for asserting that they are not understood — that they cannot be seen to be true, or at least to be truth-claims, by a non-sensory intellectual intuition? It is arbitrary, it will be argued, to adopt a principle which would rule out wondering about whether properties exist apart from their exemplifications or whether it is true that for something to have a more than conceptual existence, it must be in space-time. It is unreasonable — so the argument runs — to adopt a principle which would keep one from recognising certain facts asserted by certain statements.

However, just what is at issue is whether 'Properties exist apart from their exemplifications' or 'There are non-conceptual realities which do not exist in space-time' are actually genuine factual assertions. The empiricist could respond that nothing has been sufficiently well specified by such utterances so that something actually counts as 'recognising something to be true or false' in such contexts. Since this is so, talk of 'non-sensory intuition' vis-à-vis such claims is merely a *flatus vocus*. There is no agreement or even near-agreement about what would or would not constitute such an intuition. A claims an intuition that properties exist

68

unexemplified. B maintains that he intuits that all properties must be exemplified. No matter how much they talk of their claims' being objective, if there is no way of even having an inkling whose claim is correct, we can hardly claim to have much, if anything, in the way of an understanding of them.

To the extent that we are confident that one or another of these strange 'unverifiable satements' is true, we are construing them analytically. The man, for example, who is confident that all properties must have exemplifications is a man who construes 'property' in such a way that to be a property is by definition to be a property of something, so that it follows from the very meaning of 'property' that all properties must have exemplifications. And whether this does obtain for the word 'property' and its cognates in other languages is itself something which is open to empirical investigation. There is no need to talk of 'non-sensory intuitions' here or to think we have a genuine counter-example to verficationist claims.

Note, moreover, that, that bit of God-talk apart, my sample utterances are very deviant utterances — hardly utterances which have a use in some natural discourse. We cannot be confident that we know how to employ them in discourse or that they have a rule-governed employment. (This, by the way, is a reason for being sceptical about their putative analyticity.) But *if* they are so deviant that they are not even in accordance with the basic linguistic regularities of English, quite apart from the verifiability criterion of factual significance, it is very questionable whether they have any meaning more determinate than a vague pictorial meaning. To claim an understanding of them is precarious indeed and to claim they are statements of fact is utterly preposterous. Yet if the only parallel utterances to God-talk are such deviant utterances — utterances which are not part of any form of life — and if (other than non-anthropomorphic God-talk and witch-talk and the like) all factual discourse in form-of-life-based discourse is discourse whose truth-claims are at least in principle empirically (experientially) confirmable or infirmable, then non-anthropomorphic God-talk, which, as Wisdom points out, is suspect anyway, is surely put — vis-à-vis its factual intelligibility — in a questionable light, i.e. one can have legitimate doubts about whether such talk makes sense (24).

If Plantinga replies to this line of argument that religious and theological statements are unique — they do not have 'the logic' of other statements of fact — then he has, in this move of desperation, fallen back on what John Wisdom has appropriately called the 'idiosyncrasy platitude', namely that 'every mode of discourse has its own logic'. But from this platitude it does not follow that all modes of discourse are in order just as they are or that they are insulated from each other or that criteria of appraisal either do not or should not be adopted which cut across the different modes of discourse. We must beware of becoming the unwitting guardians of convention in simply treating it as something beyond question that all forms of life or all modes of discourse are coherent and remain in order just as they are.

We must not simply assume that if a given mode of discourse departs form other pervasive and conceptually less perplexing and more massively accepted modes of discourse, that all the same it must be conceptually beyond reproach. Perhaps it is, but that cannot be settled without examination. We must not forget that language is a structure with a history, that new concepts arise and old concepts are altered or undermined and that there can be rifts and clefts between different areas of discourse and that what we learn and how we come to think in one domain may radically affect how we come to think in another. We will miss this and fail to assess the relevance and even sometimes fail to note the irrelevance of concepts in one domain to concepts of another, if, sticking to the idiosyncrasy platitude, we continue to insist that each mode of discourse has a logic of its own, that is in order as it is. This must be shown in disputed areas such as religion and not just assumed. If we just assume that the forms of language are the forms of life *and* that they are all in order as they are, we as philosophers will lose our traditional role of considering 'not only the ways in which we do in fact reason, but also the ways in which we are *justified* in reasoning', and we will, in effect, as Perry Anderson has put it, give 'a massive, undifferentiated affadavit for the conceptual *status quo*' (25). Conceptions such as understanding, fact, truth, play a crucial role in all or nearly all forms of life, and given the Jew's or Christian's beliefs about their beliefs, they play a

70

crucial role here too. But believer and non-believer alike have come to feel perplexed not only by second-order religious discourse but also by first-order religious discourse itself. (Note, among other things, all the cultural uproar raised by the radical theologians. That it is for the most part confused, is not here to the point.) The temptation is to believe that key religious claims are factual claims, true or false, but when we reflect on this, for non-anthropomorphic God-talk, we do not understand what would make them true or false or even count towards establishing their truth or falsity. And thus we do not understand how or even that they actually succeed in making truth-claims. Verificationists think — and, I think, rightly — that they have an explanation of this in the fact that understanding a factual claim is linked, in the manner characterised above, with grasping what would at least in principle confirm or infirm the putative truth-claim. Perhaps empiricists are mistaken here, but then their critics should not fall back on the idiosyncrasy platitude but should show us some other way in which it could be established that we have good reasons to believe these putative factual claims are (a) genuinely factual and (b) either true or false. If Plantinga or Alston could do this, they would have undermined Flew's challenge and empiricist challenges generally. But neither they nor anyone else have accomplished that.

III

The responses to Flew's challenge we have hitherto examined have been attempts in one way or another legitimately to evade it. What remains to be done is to consider whether it can be met head on. That is, can it be shown, my earlier arguments to the contrary notwithstanding, that core non-anthropomorphic theistic claims are in principle at least confirmable or infirmable?

Ian Crombie and John Hick have both argued that they are (26). Their arguments have been made with subtlety and care and with an informed understanding of empiricist principles and empiricist critiques of religion. I have on previous occasions attempted to establish that all the same their efforts fail to meet adequately Flew's challenge

71

(27). I shall not rehearse here all my previous arguments but shall limit myself to a critical examination of Hick's arguments, since they constitute the most extended contemporary analytical attempt to meet, on empiricist grounds, the fundamental empiricist criticisms of religion with which I have been concerned. Moreover, in the second edition of his 'Faith and Knowledge' Hick has attempted to show that my previous criticisms of his attempts to establish that key theistic utterances are verifiable fail. However, Hick, or so it seems to me, has not succeeded in countering my original objections (28). But I return to this issue less in the spirit of philosophical controversy than in an attempt to re-examine whether Hick's determined and informed attempt to show that key theistic utterances are empirically verifiable succeeds.

Hick attempts to establish that the dispute between the atheist and the theist concerns not just different ways of looking at the world or differing attitudes but 'a momentous question of fact: the existence or non-existence of a transcendent divine Being' (29). And like a good empiricist, Hick believes that if this is so then their rival claims are in principle at least capable of confirmation or infirmation and thus are not factually vacuous.

It is clear enough that Hick agrees with Mascall and Plantinga, as against non-cognitivists such as Ayer and Braithwaite, that core religious utterances are truth-claims and that they are bits of fact-stating discourse — discourse making assertions about 'that which is the case' — and not just practical or non-cognitive forms of discourse (30). But he disagrees with Mascall and Plantinga in believing that these at least putative fact-stating bits of discourse must be experientially verifiable to be genuine factual claims (31). Here he sides with the empiricist critics of religion, only he believes, as they do not, that these religious utterances are experientially verifiable. He believes this while maintaining both that their manner of verification is unique and that they have a different logical status than do common-sense empirical assertions (32).

How then does Hick purport to show that 'the mode of experiencing that we call religious faith' is such that the key 'theological statements which express it are either verifiable

72

or falsifiable' (33)? To do this he develops a theory of 'eschatological verification'. This notion will enable him to argue in agreement with John Wisdom that while the existence of God is not an experimental issue, none the less, when we consider the Christian's future expectations of a life after the death of his physical body, the issue remains, if several other conditions hold as well, a genuinely *experiential* one, e.g. certain at least conceivable *future experiences* would verify the theist's claim and show that 'the choice between theism and atheism' is 'a real and not a merely empty or verbal choice' (34). But to establish that his conception of eschatological verification is a coherent and acceptable notion, Hick needs to show that verification and falsification may be asymmetrically related, that it need not be the case that all verification is at least in principle public, that it is at least intelligible to talk of surviving the death of one's physical body, and that the nature of the verification in question is in part determined by the subject-matter in question. The last conception apart, all of these conceptions are problematic indeed and Hick's particular utilisation of them has been powerfully criticised by William Bean in his 'Eschatological Verification: Fortress or Fairyland' (35). I shall, however, in the interest of economy and so as to offer as few hostages to fortune as possible, grant for the present discussion the viability of all these conceptions and ask, even assuming their viability, has Hick established that 'God governs the world' or 'God is our loving father' are verifiable statements of fact, though indeed eschatologically verifiable? I shall argue that he has not.

Hick's account of eschatological verification is not undermined by pointing out that belief in a survival of the death of one's physical body is perfectly compatible with atheism. Such a remarkable, continued and radically altered existence is compatible with atheism because it could be just a surprising natural fact. Life in a resurrection world could be as religiously ambiguous as our present life and we readily can conceive of conditions — or so Hick maintains — in such a world which would not verify theism (36).

What Hick believes he must do is to characterise at least a conceivable 'situation which points unambiguously to the existence of a living God' (37). The situations he has in mind

73

are (a) 'an experience of the fulfillment of God's purpose for ourselves, as this has been disclosed in the Christian revelation', and (b) 'an experience of communion with God as he has revealed himself in the person of Christ' (38). It is Hick's belief that 'if they occurred in conjunction with one another . . . they would assure us beyond rational doubt of the reality of God as conceived in the Christian faith' (39).

To display the empirical or experiential content of such a claim, and thus on Hick's own terms to make plain that a factual claim is being made, it is necessary to be able to say what we would have to experience in order for it to be the case that the divine purpose is fulfilled in our own experience. That is to say, we must have such an empirical description in order that people — or at least some people properly attuned — will be able to recognise, if they have it, that 'fulfillment in their own experience' (40). Yet, the characterisation of the experience to be had may well not be exact; our situation concerning eschatological verification of the deity may very well be analogous to that of a young child wondering what it would be like to be an adult. But in both situations we still have, Hick would have us believe, some vague idea of what it would be like to have the experience in question.

However, for such God-talk to be meaningful to us, we must have at least some vague empirical characterisation of what would constitute the expected religious awareness and we must in addition be able to give some empirical sense to what it would be like for 'the fulfillment of God's purpose' to be 'apprehended as the fulfillment *of God's* purpose and not simply as a natural state of affairs' (41). This is accomplished, Hick maintains, 'by an experience of communion with God as he has made himself known to men in Christ' (42). This reference to Christ is essential, Hick avers, for it is the doctrine of the incarnation which enables us to overcome the conceptual difficulties raised by Hepburn and others concerning the problem of how we could know or have reason to believe that it was *God* we had encountered. The notion of an encounter with God makes sense, Hick argues, because God has revealed himself in Christ. 'In coming to know Jesus Christ we come to know God and it is in this way that we can encounter God' (43). In a Barthian

74

manner, Hick stresses that 'Jesus' teaching about the Father is a part of that self-disclosure, and it is from this teaching (together with that of the prophets who preceded him) that the 'Christian knowledge of God's transcendent being is derived' (44). It is God's union with man in Jesus Christ which 'makes possible man's recognition of the fulfillment of God's purpose for man as being indeed the fulfillment of God's purpose for him' (45). The very presence of Christ settles that matter authoritatively and 'beyond doubt' (46).

There is a kind of conceptual difficulty in such an account which needs to be straight away faced. It concerns Hick's account of the verifying conditions of theism. Hick appears at least to assume what he needs to establish by argument to make his case for the factual meaningfulness of theistic utterances such as 'God governs the world' and 'God loves mankind'. This can best be brought out by first making and then drawing some inferences from the following distinction between a theistic sentence and a non-theistic sentence (47). A sentence is a theistic sentence if it is either a sentence of the type 'God exists' when that sentence is taken to be capable of making a theistic truth-claim, or a sentence that will only be known to be meaningful if we know that 'God exists' is meaningful and that it is at least believed it can be used to make a religious truth-claim. A sentence that we can know to be meaningful without making or at least assuming such claims, I shall call 'a non-theistic sentence'. To show without going in a vicious circle that such theistic sentences as 'God loves mankind' are segments of factually meaningful — because experientially verifiable — discourse, it would appear at least that the verifying conditions must be expressible exclusively in non-theistic sentences. If this condition does not obtain, one is in effect assuming, in the sentences utilised to make what are taken to be verifiable statements, exactly what one sets out to establish, namely that there are factually meaningful and verifiable *theistic* statements, i.e. statements made by using theistic sentences assertively.

In arguing that theistic statements are eschatologically verifiable and that this shows they have factual meaning, Hick speaks of predicted experiences which would verify these 'theistic statements'. But in doing this he is oblivious of

75

the above distinction. As Terence Penelhum rightly and cautiously observes, it is not clear 'whether Hick intends that these predicted experiences could be described in wholly non-theistic terms or not' (48). Hick does not draw such a distinction, but in failing to draw it, he fails to note that if his verifying conditions are not specified exclusively in non-theistic terms, he will not have succeeded in meeting Flew's challenge and the empiricist critiques of the truth-claims of religion. For if a man is puzzled about how 'There exists a Divine Reality' or 'God governs the world' can be a genuine truth-claim, he will (or at least should) be equally puzzled by other non-anthropomorphic theistic utterances, since they too utilise the same or at least very similar problematic religious concepts. To show that God-talk can make factual and experientially verifiable truth-claims, Hick must show how these putative theistic truth-claims are experientially verifiable by what are at least conceivable experiences characterisable in non-theistic terms. In my 'Eschatological Verification', I tried to establish that Hick fails to do this or even to indicate how it might be done (49). I do not see how or that his responses to me address themselves to that crucial point (50). But this may be my own blindness. I shall return again to the argument.

Hick tells us

> Our beliefs about God's infinite being are not capable of observational verification, being beyond the scope of human experience, but they are susceptible of indirect verification by the removal of rational doubt concerning the authority of Christ. An experience of the reign of the Son in the kingdom of the Father would confirm that authority and therewith, indirectly, the validity of Jesus' teaching concerning the character of God in his infinite transcendent nature (51).

But here we are moving in a circle of theistic sentences using theistic terms. 'Removal of rational doubt concerning the authority of Christ, i.e. the Son of God' and 'An experience of the reign of the Son in the kingdom of the Father' are parts of such theistic sentences. The sentences in which they occur are no more expressive of experientially verifiable

76

statements than is 'God is our loving father' or 'There is an omnipresent God'. In all these cases we have concepts which are too far removed from the experiential periphery to be capable of being taught ostensively or to indicate something we could directly experience. Similarly the experience of Christ could hardly give us the needed experiential anchorage for 'the kingdom of God' or 'God's purpose for man'. 'Jesus is the Christ' is not a logical identity statement because in speaking of Christ we are speaking of the Son of God. And all of Jesus' *agape* does not give us an understanding of the concept of the supernatural, though such talk of Jesus can be appropriately experiential and non-theistic, while to speak of Christ (the Son of God) as Hick actually does is to use a theistic term. Exactly the same considerations apply to the other key phrases Hick uses in trying to characterise the alleged predicted experiences. We remain always with theistic sentences utilising theistic terms: sentences which are not sufficiently asceptic doctrinally or metaphysically to be sentences capable of reporting states of affairs whose experiential truth-conditions can be stated as can 'Jesus was the son of Mary' or 'Jesus was born in Bethlehem'.

We will have as much trouble with 'Jesus is God incarnate', 'the experience of communion with God', 'the experience of God's purpose for ourselves', 'the experience of the self-disclosure of God in Christ', 'God's union with men in Christ', 'the proper final destiny of human nature' or 'the communion with God as he has made himself known to men in Christ' as we do with 'an infinite Divine Reality' or 'God loves man'. Flew-type challenges are perfectly appropriate for all of these if they are employed assertively as believers do indeed often attempt to employ them when they use them in indicative sentences. Moreover, they must be able so to employ them if 'the existence or non-existence of the God of the New Testament is [to be] a matter of fact . . . ' (52). But we have no idea at all what must be the case for it to be true or even probably true, or false or even probably false, that our lives have a final destiny or purpose. And we do not know, not even vaguely, what needs to happen for us to be able to assert correctly that a certain state of affairs is apprehended as the fulfillment of God's purpose and not simply as a natural state of affairs. We have no idea of what it

77

would be like to verify 'There is a community of persons infused by grace over whom the Son of God reigns'. Suppose, for example, a sceptic in his post-mortem life denied this and said instead that the community of persons were simply thoroughly good human beings ruled over by Jesus. And indeed further suppose that he said he could make nothing of the believer's talk that these persons were infused by grace or that they were ruled over by the Son of God. There are no experiences, actual or conceivable, post-mortem or otherwise, which would even infirm the sceptic's putative assertion and confirm the theist's. They are both equally compatible with anything and everything that could be experientially specified. Or to put it more modestly and in the form of a challenge, what is the *factual* and not *purely verbal* difference between these two claims? I cannot see that Hick, for this case or for cases like this, has given us grounds for thinking that the difference is, as he would have it, a real difference as to the religious facts rather than just being a verbal and, in most instances anyway, an attitudinal difference.

Similar things should be said concerning all his alleged 'predicted experiences' which are claimed to be eschatologically verifiable. None of them is stated in terms which make the putative statements, allegedly characterising it experientially, verifiable. Thus Hick has failed to achieve what he has set out to achieve with his eschatological verification, namely to establish that core theistic statements are actually factual statements open to experiential verification. Moreover, it should be noted that these criticisms do not at all turn on any claim or assumption on my part that for 'God' to be intelligible, or the concept of God coherent in the manner Hick requires, we must be able 'to state in full what it is for God to be real' or to 'set forth the *complete* truth-conditions of "God exists" . . . ' (53). Rather they are designed to establish that it has not been shown how core putative statements utilising God-talk are experientially verifiable at all, i.e. confirmable or infirmable, such that we can distinguish, even under any conceivable experientially specifiable circumstances, between the non-anthropomorphic theist's putative claim and the atheist's either with respect to their truth or falsity or their probable truth or falsity. It is not that I am contending that we must fully know what

'God' means before we can be justified in making theistic truth-claims; what I am taking to be essential is that we have some idea of what it would be like for such alleged truth-claims to be either true or false or probably true or false, and what I am claiming is that neither believers nor non-believers have a sufficient understanding of that problematic concept God to make truth-claims in or by using it. In that way 'God exists' is not at all analogous to 'Sartre is alive' (54).

IV

The discussion in section III, as well as much of my prior discussion, may provoke the objection that its surface viability is no viability at all, for my key points rest insecurely on a myth-eaten empiricist conception of language. That is to say, I have been operating with a radically oversimplified view of language and with a thoroughly misleading picture of the relation between language and the world. If we abandon this myth-eaten conception of language — still operating out of the legacy of logical empiricism — it is not so evident, some have thought, that Christianity and Judaism do not succeed in making distinctive truth-claims (55).

Some of the central considerations here are these. Such empiricist critiques of religion operate with an unrealistic ideal of empirical knowledge. Empirical statements, which form the evidential base of science and much of common sense, are regarded by such empiricists as unproblematically true or false while their religious counterparts, if they are to be coherent truth-claims at all, must, on the one hand, be either capable of being known to be true or false in the same unproblematic way or, on the other, be shown to be in some not too tenuous sense derivative from empirical statements or known to be true or false because we know certain unproblematic empirical statements to be true or false. In many standard circumstances the truth-value of 'The sun is shining' or even 'On a mountain hike obese people tire more readily than people of normal weight' is quite unproblematic while 'God looks after his creation' is not. But — the objection continues — such empirical claims are not so transparently true or false and language does not divide up in such a simple fashion. There are no firm distinctions between literal and metaphoric uses of language, between evaluative and descriptive uses of language or between descriptive and interpretative uses of language. It is not true, as the empiricist myth would have us believe, that when functioning in statements, so-called descriptive and designative words provide us with a literal characterisation of 'what there is'. There is no such direct link between language and the world. In describing the world and in seeking a direct experiential base for our descriptions we should come to realise that there can be no 'direct seeing' or 'direct experiencing'; *all* seeing is 'seeing as' and all experiencing is 'experiencing as', such that in characterising what we experience — our links with the world — there is always interpretation and we never reach a situation where we have literal description without interpretation (56). It is true, as we saw when we discussed mystical experience, that there are levels of interpretation and that some accounts of what we experience are more theologically and metaphysically ramified than others, but — or so the argument runs — we never reach a level of 'pure description' where we can without interpretation simply literally describe how things are.

The thrust of this kind of objection concerning the 'mythology of empiricist theories of language' can be developed in another way in accordance with certain strands in the work of Wilfrid Sellars (57). Sellars writes in such a way that his work is not readily accessible, for his manner of writing is intolerably obscure. He surely needs in his writing something of the manner of a Moore or a Malcolm, but for all of that — for all his need of a translator — his work is powerful and original and it provides a profound challenge to the kind of empiricism I have characterised and defended. Sellars develops in a very fundamental and distinctive way the claim that the relation between words and the world is not nearly as direct as empiricists would have it. He argues that even such terms as 'denote', 'stand for', 'truth' and 'fact'

80

are not expressive of concepts which express a word—world relation. Facts about the world, he argues, are facts only within a particular language-game; there is no language-invariant concept of fact. Indeed Sellars would agree with Zeno Vendler that facts cannot be spatially or temporally located and that talk of statements or propositions 'corresponding to' or 'fitting the facts' can, if it means anything sensible at all, only refer to consistency or harmony with the facts. But they do not refer to any putative relationship between language and the world. If for some language — say English, referred to below by Sellars as 'E' — one says '"Plato" (in E) denotes the teacher of Aristotle' this does not really make a word—world reference but actually needs to be understood as claiming that for some use (sense), S, of 'Plato' (in E), 'Plato' (in E) stands for S and is materially equivalent to 'the teacher of Aristotle' if and only if for all x, x is S if and only if what S stands for is the teacher of Aristotle (58). Sentences, Sellars contends, which tell us what some expression denotes never do anything more than relate the use of one expression to the use of another expression. By using such sentences to make statements, we do not transcend the language-game we are operating with and upon; that is, we do not succeed in 'getting outside' a particular language-game. We do not manage to relate words to the world or to make a non-language-game-relative-extra-linguistic reference to the world. Similarly, Sellars claims that 'true' does not stand for some obscure word-world relation in a correspondence between propositions and facts; rather to say 'S is true' is to authorise some form of inscription of the contained sentence 'S'. Thus 'true' is to be defined in terms of what is semantically assertable (59). Moreover, to assert, as Sellars does, that 'true' means 'semantically assertable' is to give to understand that for someone to employ a sentence such that it makes a true statement is for it to be a proper move within a given language-game; and what constitutes a proper move within a language-game is determined by what other moves have already been made in that language-game. But there is no 'hard data' or 'ground-floor level of truth' in which, unmediated by justifying assertions, again made in the language in question, we can have a direct confrontation

81

between, on the one hand, language or thought, and on the other, reality or the world. Truth is tested by coherence and 'true' is elliptical for 'true in a given conceptual structure'. The empiricist is quite mistaken in thinking that words are directly related to the world.

Empiricism — or at least the kind of empiricism I have defended and elucidated in setting forth these empiricist critiques of religion — need not, and indeed on my view should not, be committed to any metaphysical theory about the direct relation of language or thought to reality. Thus such an empiricist is not actually making claims which make him vulnerable to the above critiques of empiricism. (I do not deny that there are assumptions which Ayer, for example, makes which render him vulnerable to such a critique. But I am concerned to show that there is a consistent form of empiricism which is not vulnerable in that manner.)

There is much in such a critique that is paradoxical and perhaps even incoherent; yet Sellars in particular has worked out his account in a careful way such that he is not vulnerable to the charge that his account is in flagrant conflict with the plainest truisms of common sense. This is not the place to make a full-dress assessment of Sellars' work or of all the other complicated issues raised in this section. But it is incumbent on me to establish, if I can, whether or not they succeed in undermining the empiricist critiques I have characterised. It is my belief that they do not, and I shall try to establish that this is so. What I want to argue is that there are certain conceptual truisms and plain empirical considerations with which the critique of empiricism set forth in this section must be compatible. Either that critique is incompatible with them and thus absurd, or — as I believe it would be for Sellars — it is so interpreted and (perhaps) modified as to be compatible with this common sense and thus not ridiculously paradoxical. But if the latter alternative is the case, it will, I shall argue, admit elements which show that such empiricist claims as I have deployed are not myth-eaten or threatened by what is sound in such a criticism of traditional empiricism. (By 'common-sense beliefs', as will be evident from my examples, I do not mean the *Volks-weisheit* of our and neighbouring tribes, but something much more pervasive and enduring.)

82

However, I must move from programmatic statement to argument and clarificatory translation into the concrete. Important as it is to claim that the core putative statements of God-talk are truth-claims of a sort radically different from empirical statements, such as 'The sun is shining' or 'Bachelors tend to be misers', and important as it is to recognise that religious terms may have 'their own kind of meaning' or at least some distinctive uses, it remains the case that there are unproblematic examples of true or false empirical statements, while this is not the case for core religious putative truth-claims.

Difficult as it may be to give a *proper analysis* of what it means to say (i) and (ii) below are either true or false, we in certain common and specifiable circumstances can without any doubt at all correctly assert that they are true and can in other quite specifiable circumstances assert, again without any doubt at all, that they are false. Any philosophical analysis which cannot account for that and could not (where relevant) simply take it as a given is plainly inadequate. But this is hardly the case for the core bits of God-talk, (iii) and (iv) below. We are thoroughly puzzled about whether it is possible to have the slightest inkling whether they are, when employed in non-anthropomorphic religious discourses, either true or false.

(i)   The sun is shining.
(ii) On a mountain hike obese people tire more readily than people of normal weight.
(iii) God governs the world.
(iv) Jesus is God incarnate.

Thus it is not an empiricist dogma or any dogma at all to assert that there are certain empirical statements which are known to be true while nothing approximating this can be so unproblematically asserted concerning what is thought by some to be a knowledge of God.

This holds quite irrespective of what position we take concerning the neatness and justifiability of placing bits of language into the bins literal/metaphorical, descriptive/evaluative, descriptive/interpretative. Even if (i) and (ii) are said to be — surprisingly enough to me —interpretative and/or

83

metaphorical and/or evaluative, it still remains true that they are unproblematic truth-claims, while we are quite at sea concerning the truth-value of (iii) and (iv) as well as other core bits of God-talk. And remember that with God-talk we are not simply puzzled about its proper analysis, but about whether it makes any genuine religious truth-claims at all.

However, it seems to me that these putative distinctions mark important distinctions in our speech which have been exploited creatively by empiricists. They are hardly simply a product of empiricist thinking but are built, as clear paradigms illustrate, into the very logic of our language. And even if they are somehow 'language-relative' (whatever that means), they are still distinctions that are in the cluster of related natural languages in which we engage in our God-talk. Consider these paradigms.

(v)   Chesapeake Bay retrievers have brown hair while Labradors have black hair.
(vi)   The Canadian flag is red and white.

These two sentences would normally be used to make statements which are plainly descriptive and literal; they are not metaphorical, evaluative or interpretative. The following are paradigms of metaphorical, evaluative and interpretative utterances respectively.

(vii)   He tightened the knot of his argument.
(viii) He is a miserable speller.
(ix)   So many panfish surface feeding means the fishflies must be out.

To divide them up in that way is not to say that all five sentences do not normally have a statement-making, truth-claiming role. It is not to say that (viii) does not describe as well as evaluate or deny that (ix) is surely a true or false explanatory claim. Yet (v) and (vi) are obviously non-evaluative, non-interpretative and non-metaphorical. Moreover, they are thoroughly literal in the way (vii) is not, just as (x) ['He tightened the knot where the rope ends had been tied together'] is literal, as (vii) is not. In (x) 'tightened' and 'knot' refer to something readily ostensively teachable in

84

the way 'tightened' and 'knot' do not in (vii). Moreover, it is (in the normal case at any rate) by understanding the use of 'tightened' and 'knot' in sentences such as (x) that we come to grasp what (vii) is all about. When (vii) was a live metaphor, 'tightened' and 'knot' were used in unusual ways in such utterances — ways which suggested certain likenesses between certain arguments and slipping a knot tight. The novels of Virginia Woolf, for example, are replete with live and enriching metaphors that often also make remarkable descriptions and convey insight. But without a base of quite literal, straightforwardly descriptive utterances such as (v) and (vi), it would not be possible to have metaphorical utterances. There are surely many blends and disputable cases and there is more metaphor even in science than most philosophers and scientists recognise, but without a range of clearly literal cases, metaphor would not be possible. The same considerations apply even more obviously to interpretative utterances and purely descriptive utterances. In both cases, for the conceptions to be intelligible, we need a non-vacuous contrast.

Compare 'Hitler had black hair', 'Hitler had a black soul' and 'Hitler was a vile man'. The first utterance is plainly value-neutral and the latter two are plainly evaluative with the second one in the trio also being metaphorical. It is a mistake to think that such distinctions are not built into the logic of our language. Moreover, for us to have some confidence in whether (vii), (viii), (ix), 'Hitler had a black soul' and 'Hitler was a vile man' are true rather than false or false rather than true, we need to know the truth or falsity or probable truth or probable falsity of many literal empirical statements of type (v) or (vi). Thus such empirical statements indeed have a 'ground-floor' position in human discourse. To make such distinctions and to recognise the centrality of plain matter-of-fact empirical statements in human discourse is not to be caught up in an empiricist myth, rather it is to stick stubbornly and realistically to very pervasive common-sense considerations.

Thus it is a mistake to asert that there is no literal description without interpretation. There is no interpretation in (vi), for example; that is to say, there is nothing comparable to what goes on in (ix). In (vi) there is neither explanation, as in (ix), nor interpretation as in 'Much of Max Beekman's work depicts the dehumanisation of man'. Similar considerations hold for the claim that all seeing is and indeed must be seeing—as and Hick's expansion of it to all experiencing is experiencing—as (60). The truth of the matter is that only if there is or at least could be some plain seeing, could there be any seeing—as at all. I could noly see the famous duck-rabbit figure as a duck and as a rabbit, if I knew what it would be like to see a duck and a rabbit. If I have seen (directly observed) ground squirrels and small stumps, I might in a mountain meadow where there are many ground squirrels and small stumps mistake a stump for a ground squirrel and vice versa. After recognising my error, I might say to my companion who had not made that error, 'Look at it from this angle. Doesn't it look like a ground squirrel?' and he might come to see what he *knew* to be a stump as a ground squirrel. But it is only possible to see x as y if it is possible both just to see x and just to see y. To see or experience an x as a y presupposes an acquaintance with y's. It would be impossible for anyone to see anything as a ground squirrel unless he had seen ground squirrels, pictures of ground squirrels, had been told what he would have to see to see a ground squirrel, or something of that order. If it is not possible to see ground squirrels, it would not be possible *to see* something else *as a* ground squirrel. 'Seeing-as' and 'experiencing-as' is conceptually parasitical on 'seeing' and 'experiencing'. Thus, if this argument is correct, it will be impossible justifiably to maintain, as Hick (for example) wants to, that all seeing is seeing-as and all experiencing is experiencing-as (61). Moreover, we cannot take the believer's claim to have an awareness of God, to have a sense of the presence of God, to non-inferentially know God or to have had an encounter with God as something which could be elucidated in terms of 'experiencing life as a continual interaction with the transcendent God', for since we — believer and non-believer alike — do not know what it would be like to experience God (see him, hear him, touch him, be aware of him and the like), talk of 'experiencing-as' here is without meaning. To see anything as x or to experience anything as x, it is at least necessary to know what it would be like to see x or to experience x. This can be done with rabbits, ducks and ground squirrels, as well as with thoughts and feelings, but not with God. (We cannot even be aware of God as we are aware of a feeling.) Thus if we do not understand, as we do not, what it would be like to be directly aware of or directly to encounter God, we cannot intelligibly assert, as Hick does, that there are 'two contrasting ways of experiencing the events of our lives and of human history, on the one hand as purely natural events and on the other hand as mediating the presence and activity of God' (62).

It has been maintained that empiricist critiques of religion are undermined because they fail to note and draw the proper inferences from the claims that all description involves interpretation, all seeing is seeing-as and all experiencing is experiencing-as (63). What I have said is, I think, sufficient to refute these claims, but I am tolerably confident that it will leave some people at least with a lingering sense of dissatisfaction. Something, it will be felt, has been left out. What I think this attests to is that behind these mistaken doctrines and confused with them are some crucial conceptual points. One is that there are indefinitely large numbers of alternative descriptions of what are confusedly or at least paradoxically called 'the same event' or 'the same situation or occurrence'. Someone hears a splash in the water. I say 'It's a trout surface feeding'. But it could be said 'It's a fish jumping', 'A trout made a splash', 'A trout came out of the water', 'A speckled fish came to the surface', 'A fish made a big noise', 'Something came out of the water', and the like. There are no criteria for a kind of 'brute description' which just minimally describes what happened, though indeed some descriptions are 'bruter' than others, e.g. 'A small cut-throat trout jumped' is bruter than a 'A fish jumped'. But the crucial thing to see is that there are always alternative descriptions possible. But while it is true that many of them, in certain contexts could also serve as interpretations, they could not all serve as interpretations simultaneously, for only if there is something which is just described and not interpreted and only if there are some data which we just refer to in description but do not in that context interpret, could anything even count as 'an interpretation', for we interpret something which we can independently describe and we check our interpretations by

87

an appeal to data which are again specifiable and describable independently of the interpretation.

Similarly, while it is the case (as Hick stresses) that that which affects the retina can be consciously perceived in different ways that does not establish that all seeing is seeing-as or even that in a given case seeing-as is going on. Such an awareness of multiple perspectives may be *necessary* for seeing-as, but it is not *sufficient*. It usually happens when people look at Jastrow's duck-rabbit and such figures, but when I see a fork and a man from a more primitive culture only sees a shiny hard object, I do not see a fork as a fork and he does not see what he sees as a something. Rather we have different classificatory systems, different cultural categories and different background beliefs. We cannot equate 'seeing-as' with 'visual recognition' or 'experiencing-as' with 'recognising'. When I recognise Smith in a crowd, I do not see him as Smith. Rather I see Smith, though if someone I recognised to be Smith were dressed in a carnival costume during carnival time, I might see Smith as, say, Mephistopheles. But again seeing-as would always be parasitical on seeing.

Thus we should not try to collapse the conceptual distinction between 'seeing' and 'seeing-as', even though we should acknowledge the different claim that to identify an object, as we do when we see something, involves conceptualising it, that is categorising it, in certain ways. That is to say, when I see an object in the sky and say it is a hawk, I make all kinds of implicit claims about its shape, structure, size, about its past and about its future behaviour. Seeing is not a mere automatic registering of what is on the retina; it involves many socially mediated conceptualisations. But this does not mean that when I see a hawk in the sky, I am seeing it as a hawk; and it does not mean or at all justify the claim that all seeing is seeing-as.

One might abandon this attempt at collapsing interpretation and describing, seeing-as and seeing, as being pointlessly paradoxical and still maintain, as Hick does, that 'all conscious perceiving goes beyond what the senses report to a significance which has not been given to the senses' (64). Thus some are said to be conscious of God when in solitude 'the divine presence is borne in upon them by the vastness

88

of the starry heavens above or the majestic beauty of a
sunrise or a mountain range . . . . ' (65). When their eyes are
turned (for example) to a vast mountain range – say the
Jungfraujoch – certain things are happening to their retinas
and there are features of the mountain range that they can
point to and (if need be) they can ostensively teach the
words in their language designating and describing them. But
we are not conscious of God in that same direct way or even
in a similar way; we do not become aware of God as we
become aware of a glacier. Our awareness of God, Hick tells
us (and here he surely speaks as many believers would), is 'an
awareness in our experience as a whole of a significance
which transcends the scope of the senses' (66). But here God,
as something which transcends that which is 'given to the
senses', transcends 'what is given to the senses' in a very
different way than does a glacier. As Wisdom would put it,
the logic of 'God' and the logic of 'glacier' are very different.

We can by a mixture of verbal and ostensive teaching, with
ostension playing a very fundamental role, teach the
difference between 'glacier', 'icefield' and 'snow on the
mountains'. But 'God' is in no way so ostensively teachable.
There is nothing in the way of ostensive teaching that would
enable us to distinguish between what (if anything) either
disputant was actually asserting when, in the face of the same
observables, actual and conceivable, they tried to assert either
a or a| and/or b or b|.

a. He was aware of God when he contemplated the earth's
   marvellously varied face.
a|.He was not aware of God but was only aware of a
   feeling of awe and a feeling of utter finitude when he
   contemplated the earth's marvellously varied face.
b. He saw Jesus as the Christ (the son of God).
b|.He saw Jesus, not as the Christ (the son of God), but
   only as a profoundly inspired moral leader.

In this way, a and a| and b and b| are very unlike 'He saw a
glacier' and 'He only saw an icefield'. We understand with the
latter what is being asserted and denied and how to go about
establishing which claim is correct and which is not. a and a|
and b and b| are, by contrast, both sets of putatively factual

statements which are equally compatible with anything and everything that might conceivably impinge on our retinas. And here, to repeat, is the essential difference, for this is not true of 'He saw a glacier' and 'He only saw an icefield'. We have some understanding of the truth-conditions of the latter set of claims while this is not at all true for the religious utterances.

Even if my arguments so far are sound, it may well be thought that I have yet to face the most powerful impediments to the viability of my account: to wit, the strands of Sellars's thought I have sketched. The claim — now rather a commonplace — that there is no direct non-conventional relationship between language and the world seems to me correct and it may even be that 'denote', 'stand for', 'truth' and 'fact' are not expressive of concepts which signify a word-world relation. Sentences which tell us what some expression denotes may never do anything more than relate the use of one expression to another, though it does seem to me that what Sellars says about the coneptual-scheme relativity of truth and fact is at least counter-intuitive. Similar considerations hold for his attempt to define 'true' as 'being semantically assertable'. But he does make some powerful arguments for these paradoxical claims.

Sellars realises the paradoxical nature of his contentions and as a scientific realist he wants to maintain that the conceptual structures of science are superior to those of other forms of life: that science gives us a more adequate conception of reality than do other conceptual structures (67). His own remarks about picturing are an attempt to break out of a conceptual relativism which would vitiate his scientific realism. In trying to make this break Sellars is driven — much in the manner of some empiricists — to an attempt to conceive of the marks constituting the inscriptions of basic empirical sentences as standing in a picturing relation to the objects of the world. He takes 'picturing' to be a complex matter of fact relation functioning very differently than do 'denotation' and 'truth' (68). Sellars argues that a break with conceptual relativism is justified by the fact that certain conceptual structures, certain language-games, picture more adequately than others. With these methods of picturing different words are related, more or less adequately, to the world.

However, Sellars seems quite at a loss to provide us with criteria of adequacy for picturing or mapping. It is far from clear how it is possible or even that it is possible to describe objects which are no more the objects of one given language-game than any other. What is taken as an object and how it is to be characterised, what is taken as a fact, seems always to be delimited by a given language. To do what Sellars wants to do, we need a vocabulary which is common to all language-games. Sellars thinks that certain purely formal aspects of logical syntax will enable us 'to form the concept of a domain of objects' in a way which abstracts from particular aspects of natural languages and specific conceptual structures (69). But the criteria here remain too thin: we only have criteria for individuality and for n-adic and m-adic predicates. But this will hardly tell us whether scientific discourse maps more adequately than religious discourse or the various other forms of everyday discourse or whether the language-games of one culture are superior to those of another. With his notion of picturing, he clearly wants to show how language can make an extra-linguistic reference; but his characterisation is too amorphous to be a very helpful guide. However, he does recognise that without it his account would stand as a rank paradox.

It even seems to me doubtful whether we can find an artificial language or set of linguistic categories, neutral between language-games, for specifying the objects that Sellars says language pictures. Yet it remains the case that certain conceptions in certain language-games can be seen to be more adequate than others. Even if 'facts' are always characterised intra-linguistically, there remains a crucial difference between the first pair of presumptive 'fact-specifications' and the second.

First Pair:

' "Satan" denotes the Devil.'
'. "God" denotes the maker of the world.'

Second Pair:

'"Edmonton" denotes the Capital of Alberta.'
'"Winston Churchill" denotes the war-time
Prime Minister of England.'

With the first pair we never break out of a charmed linguistic circle. With them there is nothing extra-linguistic being successfully talked about for the linguistic expressions to be related to and, unlike 'the present king of Hungary', there is not even anything specifiable in the way of experience in virtue of which the expressions of the first pair *could* be so related. But this is not true for the expressions of the second pair. Given some tolerable understanding of English, these expressions can have their meaning specified through ostensive teaching. And this ensures that they have extra-linguistic relations; that they make a link, however indirect and conventional, with the world. But where we have putative referring expressions and no such link, where there is no such possiblity of either direct or indirect ostensive teaching, we have incoherence, for there is no way of knowing whether the alleged truth-claims, however conceptually relative, are either true or false. But this leads us back to empiricism again and to empiricist criteria of factual intelligibility, i.e. truth-claims about what there is.

Even if we accept Sellars's account, such a distinction can and indeed should be drawn. When we think through the crucial differences between the above two pairs, we come to see how some terms have extra-linguistic relations and how others do not, even though the surface grammar of the terms that do not are such that prior to inquiry (that is inquiry about such terms) one would expect that they had extra-linguistic relations. Such a recognition of the centrality in such contexts of ostensive teaching and thus of experience gives us a better hint concerning a method by which we might appraise the adequacy of conceptual systems making putative claims about what there is than does the obscure notion of picturing. To argue in this way is not at all to be committed to some empiricist 'myth of the given' and it helps vindicate empiricist critiques of religion or at least shows how they have nothing to fear from such Sellarian notions.

To sum up the thrust of this chapter, I have tried to show

that what has been dubbed Flew's challenge is a genuine challenge indeed and that it has not been met or successfully by-passed. Core religious utterances purport to be truth-claims, yet they fail to make intelligible truth-claims. The critiques of religion coming out of the empiricist tradition have given us good grounds for believing that the key claims of anthropomorphic God-talk are false and that non-anthropomorphic God-talk — the talk of the dominant tradition of Judaism and Christianity — is so incoherent that no intelligible truth-claim is actually made by these putative truth-claims.

In following out the dialectic of the arguments for and against this contention, we saw something of the claims of conceptual relativism. I want to show in the next chapter that even if this tantalising thesis of conceptual relativism can be shown to be coherent, and even if it is true, the implications for religion cut in the direction of religious scepticism and not in the direction of fideism.

5 The Challenge of Conceptual Relativism

In the preceding chapters I have explained and defended an empiricist critique of religion designed to establish that the central doctrines of Judaism, Christianity and Islam — the most fundamental religious and theological claims which these forms of life presuppose — do not succeed in making intelligible truth-claims. However, I should report, as an informed though impressionistic sociological generalisation about philosophers, that I am in the minority here and that at present most analytic philosophers, even those nurtured in a tradition which took verificationism very seriously, do not believe that even the weakened and restricted version of the verifiability principle I have espoused will carry the critical weight I have given it. Philosophers influenced primarily by Quine and/or Goodman, on the one hand, or Wittgenstein and/or Wisdom, on the other, look with very considerable suspicion on such verificationist arguments. They are frequently felt to be, depending on how they are made, either bold mistakes or truistic claims which will not do the work expected of them.

It is not at all unusual to find philosophers as well as theologians oriented towards linguistic analysis claiming that this phase of the discussion about the intelligibility of God-talk is or at least should be over: that the verificationist challenge has been met or at least broken and that discussions concerning God-talk have entered a new phase (1).

Linked with this rejection of verificationism, there is also a very widespread conviction among analytic philosophers of both a Quinean and a Wittgensteinian colouring that any belief in what has been called a metaphysics of hard facts indifferent to the conventions of our language rests on an illusion. In fact, such a belief is itself an incoherent bit of metaphysics. There is no escaping our lingua-centric predicament. To think or understand anything at all we must

94

simply start with a socially inherited framework, i.e. a language with its rules and regulations. This linguistic framework determines for its users what it makes sense to say, determines all nomological relations between statements, whether analytic or empirical, and indeed what in that linguistic framework is to count as 'analytic' or 'empirical'. Ayer, verificationist that he is, shows his sensitivity to such conceptions of linguistic or, if you will, conceptual frameworks in the following remarks:

> I believe in science. That is, I believe that a theory about the way the world works is not acceptable unless it is confirmed by the facts, and I believe that the only way to discover what the facts are is by empirical observation. At the same time I do not think that the distinction between theory and fact is altogether sharp. What we count as a fact is to some extent a function of our theories and even more a function of the system of concepts which are embodied in our language. The world exists independently of our perceiving it or thinking about it, but the world of which we can significantly speak — and *ex hypothesi* it makes no sense to speak of their being any other — is moulded to the linguistic or, if you prefer, conceptual framework which makes it possible for us to speak about it. This form of relativity is inescapable. It is conceivable that we should employ a different conceptual system, but it is not possible for us to view the world in detachment from any conceptual system whatsoever. To this extent, the idealists were right. But it is because of the objective features of the world that our concepts can be successfully applied to it (2).

The first two sentences — sentences which we also quoted for another purpose in another context in an earlier chapter — are entirely in the tenor of his verificationism. But with the third sentence we get a complicating factor relevant to our present context. If we drop Ayer's qualifier 'to some extent', we get the kind of conceptual relativism I shall discuss. (In section II of the last chapter I, in effect, mentioned some difficulties in one form of it. But none the less it remains a plausible position and it is crucial to come to recognise its

95

import in philosphical discussions of religion.) To be such a conceptual relativist is to argue that what is to count as knowledge, evidence, truth, a fact, an observation, making sense and the like is uniquely determined by the linguistic framework used and that linguistic frameworks can and do radically vary. What we can know about the world and what we will take to be intelligible and the basic facts in the case is completely moulded by the linguistic framework we use. Moreover, it is an ethnographic fact and a linguistic truism that there are different conceptual systems with radically different conceptions of intelligibility, validity, rationality, knowledge, truth, value and the like. But since our very conceptions of intelligibility, validity, knowledge and the like are a function of the linguistic system we use, it is impossible for us to attain a neutral Archimedean point in virtue of which we could evaluate the comparative adequacy of our own and other linguistic frameworks. Conceptual relativism is inescapable; we are caught in a lingua-centric predicament and in claiming superiority for our own linguistic framework we are — inescapably — simply being ethnocentric.

Such a conclusion is indeed distressing, but like it or not, it is, as Ayer puts it, impossible 'to view the world in detachment from any conceptual system whatsoever'. We can — though indeed with difficulty — come to adopt another system or modify our linguistic system. The latter, as Wittgenstein observed, constantly goes on, but we cannot transcend our own and all linguistic systems and independently of any system take note of data which will check the adequacy of our own system or any other system or enable us to rank the systems or ascertain what reality is like independently of all linguistic frameworks. We may criticise one conceptual framework in terms of another, but such appraisals, such reflections of the critical spirit, are always question-begging.

Ayer seems to escape the full brunt of the thrust of conceptual relativism by his qualifier that what is to count as 'a fact' is in large measure, but not completely, a function of our linguistic framework. He further qualifies such relativism with his talk of 'objective features of the world', which are supposedly there to be taken note of by any linguistic framework that sought completeness and full explanatory power. But it is at least natural to argue that these qualifications are ill-thought-out evasions, for our linguistic framework determines all nomological relations between statements, whether formal, causal or epistemic. The linguistic framework we operate with warrants the acceptance of statements as well as inferences. Within our present linguistic framework, we may indeed be completely justified in accepting a given statement, but with a change in linguistic framework, what superficially at least appears to be the same statement might become unwarranted.

Even what we know from observation will depend on the linguistic framework we are using. For what counts as our basic empirical data will be a function of that framework. There is no point at which, framework free, there is some direct observation of the facts — some conceptually unmoulded confrontation with our world. What will count as an observation statement unavoidably bears the conceptual scars of this relativity. Our very statements of observation — our records of observable fact — are as subject to rejection or revision through a change in our linguistic framework as any other statements. What counts as 'the objective features of the world' is a function of the linguistic framework we have adopted.

Conceptual relativists will point out that I have adopted — as has Ayer and other empiricist critics of religion — a framework in which there can be no direct knowledge of God and in which fundamental religious propositions are not even in principle verifiable. But it is perfectly possible to adopt a linguistic framework in which this is not so. And no reason has been given or can be given for adopting such an empiricist linguistic framework. Father Clarke, for example and by contrast, adopts a linguistic framework in which to speak to 'God transcending all of nature, who calls the believer to a new personal supernatural relation with him' is to make a truth-claim (3). In the linguistic framework Ayer adopts or I adopt, such an utterance does not have such a literal sense. But there is no sense in saying that we empiricists are right and Father Clarke is wrong or vice versa. Or rather (and more accurately), such remarks could be made, but only as internal statements within a particular framework. The kind of cross-framework validity desired to give such claims objective validity is impossible to attain, for the very idea of it is incoherent. We just play different language-games with different rules of formation and transformation and the like, but there is no showing one language-game to be superior to another.

Such a conceptual relativism has to date — where it has had any use in relation to religion — been employed to support the rationality or at least the propriety of religious belief and to undermine philosophical attempts to criticise it (4). This has usually taken the form of what I have called Wittgensteinian fideism and have criticised at length elsewhere; or it has, as in the work of John Wisdom, taken the form of an endless fence-straddling between belief and unbelief with a sophisticated attempt to show that philosophical criticism of religious belief and indeed all forms of scepticism are centres of confusion (5). However, such conceptual relativism can and has been used to criticise religion and it may be felt by some to be a deeper, far more fundamental form of criticism than the empiricist critiques I have examined. In a book devoted to contemporary critiques of religion, it is crucial that I examine such critiques. However, in stating and critically examining such an account, I face the difficulty that, to date, it has had no extended or careful statement. Wittgensteinian scepticism or atheism as a general methodological stance is as appropriate or inappropriate as Wittgensteinian fideism — and the same thing would apply to someone working out of a Quinean framework — but it has yet to find its D.Z. Phillips (6). I shall, because I think such a critique important and in many ways compelling, construct such a case myself, often using the arguments of Wittgensteinian fideists, for — and this is itself revealing — often with just a little twist their arguments can be turned in favour of a form of scepticism that may be very profound indeed.

II

In coming to see the force of such a position, we must first come to see the necessity of jettisoning metaphysical talk of a concept of reality which linguistic frameworks, forms of life, universes of discourse may or may not square with or correspond to. There is and can be no such concept of reality in accordance with which we rank and test our various

98

conceptual systems. Our very idea of reality is given within the particular universe of discourse we use. Our concepts there settle for us the form of experience we have of the world. 'What is real and what is unreal shows itself in the sense language has' (7). The very distinction between what is real and what is unreal and the conception of what constitutes 'an agreement with' or a 'true link with' reality is only given within a particular universe of discourse and it is relative to that universe of discourse. If we understand the rules and regularities of this discourse and the purpose or purposes it serves, we can come to understand the distinction within that particular discourse between what is real and what is not. But since the sense that 'real' and 'unreal' or 'illusion' have is given *within a particular discourse*, there can be no intelligible notion of what is reality *sans phrase*, and no intelligible conception of comparing various universes of discourse and deciding which ones make a true or truer link with reality. We can't even be agnostic here, for such notions are only disguised bits of nonsense — nothing we could have legitimate doubts about. We may feel that we have intelligible notions here, just as we may feel it makes sense to speak of its being 3 p.m. on Mars, but when we probe our language a little we recognise, or at least should recognise, that this talk is nonsensical.

Phillips maintains that critics of religion such as those we have been considering miss the above point (8). The empiricist claim is that talk of caps, rainbows and mesons makes sense while talk of God does not, for the former talk, unlike the latter, 'corresponds to an objective reality'. But here, Phillips continues, the empiricists are making the mistake of 'speaking as if there were a check on what is real and what is unreal which is *not* found in the actual use of language, but which transcends it' (9). But no sense has been or can be given to such a notion. The distinction between reality and illusion shows itself *within particular language-games*: particular modes of discourse which human beings engage in. There is no super-norm of meaningfulness or reality transcending what is found in the particular modes of discourse.

The immediate effect of an acceptance of such a conceptual relativism is that it seems to free religious belief

99

from legitimate philosophical criticism. The kind of empiricist criticisms we have been considering will be seen in a new light if such a conceptual relativism is accepted. It will then appear to be the case that the empiricist critics we have discussed as well as many other critics of religion have illegitimately taken the concept of reality (and of rationality and intelligibility as well) embedded in the scientific and common-sense modes or universes of discourse and illegitimately applied them to a quite different mode or universe of discourse, namely religious discourse. Empiricists, for example, have in effect treated 'God created the heavens and the Earth', 'He is the living God, an everlasting king' and 'The Lord is with me as a mighty terrible one: Therefore my persecutors shall stumble, and they shall not prevail' as if they were pseudo-scientific or empirical hypotheses. But this is the grossest kind of category mistake — a mistake which completely fails to understand what they do mean, and assimilates in an utterly illegitimate way two very different universes of discourse, with different criteria of reality and intelligibility. What we must recognise is that while religious discourse and scientific discourse are radically different, both are established forms of life with internally coherent linguistic frameworks and distinct but equally legitimate conceptions of reality. An empiricist critique of religious discourse is in reality nothing more than the pointless lament that religious discourse is not scientific discourse. But it is illegitimate to criticise it for something it does not even purport to be.

Wittgenstein, in his 'Lectures and Conversations on Aesthetics, Psychology and Religious Belief', drives home that point and makes incisive criticisms of both non-believers who criticise religious claims on the grounds that they are not empirical hypotheses and believers who try to defend them as if they were. Within religious discourse, as within scientific discourse, an agent's beliefs and ideas are checkable by reference to something independent of him. Thus within religious discourse Job is finally instructed and corrected by God when God speaks to him out of the whirlwind. Job is taken to task for having lost sight of the reality of God. His error, faithful believer that he was, was in thinking of God's goodness and reality as being dependent on what happens. This is a common enough *religious* mistake and it can be shown to be a mistake using the conceptions of rationality and reality embedded in the religious universe of discourse, though note that Job, in making this religious mistake, did not make any scientific or observational mistake that might be corrected by scientific experiment and testing. To try to attack the whole system of thought and belief in accordance with which Job thinks and feels and has his being is utterly senseless. It is senseless to say that scientific ideas and those common-sense ideas which are based on empirical observation make a true link with an independent reality while religious ideas do not. That such a linkage obtains cannot be shown to be true, for if 'true link' or 'independent reality' is explained by reference to the scientific universe of discourse, the question has been begged, and if we try to construe 'true link' and 'independent reality' as having a sense outside of any universe of discourse at all or as making no reference to any particular universe of discourse at all, we have (depending on how exactly it is construed) either said something which is nonsensical or something so indeterminate in meaning that it does not constitute a truth-claim.

One way to attempt to escape the full force of conceptual relativism, while still accepting the basic contention that one's framework determines one's conception of reality and intelligibility, is to argue that a linguistic framework which is scientifically oriented is a more adequate linguistic framework than the others because it more adequately meets the goal of explanatory coherence. Such a claim, favoured by Quineans (Wilfrid Sellars is a paradigm here) but hardly by Wittgensteinians (Rush Rhees being a parallel paradigmatic Wittgensteinian), takes a scientifically oriented linguistic framework to be one in which the scientific and formal (logico-mathematical) universes of discourse are taken to be the fundamental and governing universes of discourse and the religious universes of discourse are excluded or regarded as logically dispensible, non-cognitive modes of discourse. Our lives presumably are better served if we favour a linguistic framework which yields a maximum of explanatory coherence among all that turns out to be knowledge within that framework. Scientific and utterly secular linguistic frameworks score high on this test and religious ones poorly, so the scientific ones are the more adequate frameworks. The method of explanation in theoretical science is a key paradigm of explanatory methodology. By using such a method of explanation, we maximise our chances of gaining a linguistic framework which will in the most coherent fashion explain and classify everything that impinges on our sense organs. Our knowledge of the world does not guide our choice of linguistic framework because nothing can ever count as knowledge except in terms of a linguistic framework. But to achieve the maximum explanatory coherence of that blooming, buzzing confusion that constitutes the having of a sensory life, we should adopt such a scientifically oriented linguistic framework and exclude religious and transcendental conceptions. The goal of such explanatory coherence is the overriding goal of human rationality. Thus the knowledge claims of science should be warranted by the rules of our linguistic framework at the expense of all conflicting claims.

This pragmatic vindication of the scientific-secular frame of reference seems to me very shaky indeed. The most obvious points are that human beings have many diverse purposes and needs, some theoretical and some non-theoretical. Maximising explanatory coherence is only one among many distinctively human goals and it is very questionable whether it is the overridingly important end of human endeavour. Even in trying to gain a sense of the significance of human life, it does not, as Winch brilliantly shows, play the most central role (10). Furthermore, to take the achievement of such explanatory coherence as the over-riding goal of human rationality is thoroughly ethnocentric and question-begging. It also, I should think, shows little insight in to what constitutes a human life. I shall not try to argue that latter point but I shall argue the former. Such a conceptualisation of rationality is ethnocentric and question-begging, for even in terms of our forms of language and forms of life, to say nothing of our primitive contemporaries, it selects a single conception of rationality and takes this as the sole and governing criterion of rationality. It neglects the fact that just as what is taken to constitute reality, knowledge and evidence is determined by one's linguistic framework, so what is taken to constitute rationality is also determined by one's linguistic framework. In short, there are differing conceptions of rationality with different centres of interest. What has been done here by such 'scientific realists' in such a defence of the 'Scientific World Outlook' (or, if you will, 'onlook') is simply to assume the criterion of rationality of their own particular linguistic framework and then to use it to establish the superiority of their framework. But this is to go around in a small and vicious circle. The point is that there are purposes and purposes, and a multitude of language-games and forms of life. No adequate pragmatic vindication has been given for giving the 'Scientific World Perspective' pride of place. Such argument for it as we have just outlined is hardly more than a fancy way of treating science as a sacred cow.

III

Conceptual relativism, if indeed it is a correct account of what it makes sense to say and of how in the end we settle ultimate questions, may save religion from empiricist and 'scientific realist' attacks, through establishing that religious discourses are conceptually autonomous and have their own distinctive order and rationales with their own distinctive conceptions of reality, rationality, knowledge, evidence, intelligibility and the like. But such a 'salvation' may pave the way for its ultimate destruction or utter transformation.

Suppose it is the case, as many conceptual relativists argue, that the meaning of a word either is its role in the language or that to understand the meaning of a word is to come to grasp its role in the language. Assume further that the same thing or very nearly the same thing is to be said for sentences. In short, the meaning of such linguistic units is determined by their role in the language and is a function of the rules of language (the linguistic framework) of which they are a part. God-talk, like all other universes of discourse, has its distinctive uses based on the rules of language of the religious mode of discourse.

It is not that there is such a thing as religious language, for there is not, but there are religious uses of language with their own distinctive regularities; and this universe of discourse, like all other universes of discourse, has its own distinctive rationale. And to discover what it is, we must discover the major centres of interest connected with religion and discover what distinctive jobs God-talk does when it is employed in religious contexts. To progress here we must regard actual *speech* where words are clearly functioning as part of an ongoing practice (form of life). There we see that in learning God-talk we are learning to play one of a myriad of language-games, namely, a whole consisting of language and the actions into which it is woven. Our linguistic framework is our ensemble of language-games. It is in them that we come to see the work words do and the roles they play. It is here where we have our diverse criteria for what it makes sense to say. And with the recognition of this, the absurdity of searching for overall criteria of meaningful discourse becomes manifest. There are countless different kinds of uses of language, countless numbers of evolving and changing language-games. The criterion for the meaningful employment of any expression is context-dependent. What it will be is determined by the word's or sentence's role in a given language-game. It is there in the particularity of a given context that we find criteria for what it makes sense to say and even what it is rational to claim. There are these forms of life which our language-games reveal. They differ radically, but there is no 'one big language-game' or archetypal rule or set of rules of language in accordance with which we can appraise language-games or form general criteria for intelligibility and rationality. God-talk is one particular form of language-game, or more particularly Christian-talk, Judaic-talk and Islamic-talk are particular language-games self-contained and immune to exterior criticism with a distinctive logic (style of functioning) of their own.

But if this is the case, then Christian-talk is but one language-game among a myriad of language-games. It can have — given such a conceptual relativism — no legitimate claim to a superior reality or deeper truth or profounder insight than any other language-game. It is a legitimate form of language; that is, participants in this language-game know how to go on with it in varied circumstances. However, this is also true for Zande witchcraft-talk, Haitian voodoo-talk,

104

Dobuan talk of sacred yams, Apa Tani talk of the Land of the Dead and the like. Unless and until a language-game breaks down in practice, it is perfectly in order, perfectly intelligible and rational as it is. To criticise it from outside – from some different linguistic framework – is simply a mistake resting on a failure to understand what it is for a discourse to be intelligible. Christian-talk, given such a conception, has its own perfectly legitimate order, but it can also in no objective sense be a claim to be the truth about man or to be the way and the life if man is to gain salvation. Given the truth of conceptual relativism, such Christian-talk could in the very nature of the case have no objective rationale. Part of Christian training teaches us to say and believe that Christ is the truth and the way, the deepest and profoundest and perhaps the only true road of salvation. Indeed, when these utterances are uttered by a believer, they have a commissive force. In their very sincere avowal, they commit their avower to a certain norm in virtue of which he attempts to regulate his life and in accordance with which he makes his appraisals of the significance of human life. But they also have a constative force in that they allegedly make fundamental truth-claims about the nature of reality. But if the conceptual relativist account about meaning and what it is to speak of reality is correct, no such general statements, as Christian-talk seems at least to commit us to, could make sense. This part of the theist's talk must be judged to be idle talk. Given the truth of conceptual relativism, there can be no such general statements about the nature of reality. We cannot succeed in making statements about reality *überhaupt*, but only about the realities of a particular situation.

To this it will be replied that indeed such Christian-talk cannot sensibly be taken to be making statements about the nature of reality as such or about the nature of 'ultimate reality'. Such talk is in a pejorative sense metaphysical. However, since it does not make sense, it cannot be correct to say, as we just have, that Christian-talk or any other language-game commits us to making such problematic claims. Christian-talk is not like much metaphysical-talk, talk which neither constitutes a language-game nor a part of a language-game. Rather, we do with Christian-talk have a

105

language-game that is part of an ongoing form of life and so, if the above account of language and meaning is correct, it must be perfectly intelligible talk. Only we must not construe it as metaphysical-talk about all of reality or ultimate reality, for such talk has no foundation in any language-game and can have no foundation in any language-game, for it is trying to say what cannot be said, i.e. what reality is like in itself independently of the assumption of the distinctive norms of intelligibility, rationality and reality of particular language-games.

As an ex-participant, I think that I — like most other people in our culture — have something of a grasp of how Christian-talk works. I can, as quickly as a Christian, spot deviant uses of this talk, and I can go on in this language-game as readily as he can. With this typical training in this form of life, it seems to me evident enough, as it does to many others as well, that 'Christ is the truth and the way' is such a metaphysical remark. But even dropping the claim that this is the way it is to be understood, in deference to those participants who do not construe it in this way, the problem remains: Construe it as you will, if you are also construing it in accordance with conceptual relativist conceptions about meaning and criteria for rationality, it could not be making a truth-claim superior to or profounder than that built into any of the other myriad of conflicting religious language-games or secularist language-games. Nor could it be in any way superior to those language-games which are simply different. The forms of language are the forms of life. But the forms of life are varied as are their attendant conceptions of rationality, intelligibility and truth.

In defending the intelligibility and coherence of God-talk — including Christian-talk — an appeal is made by some believers who are philosophically in Wittgenstein's corner to the rock-bottom fact that this language-game is played. Its very existence as an ongoing form of life with such truth-claims as central elements in it shows its invulnerability. But such a defence is the kiss of death, for the clear realisation of such a relativity and such a limitation of what religious claims can come to will produce a scepticism that, where the insight is keen, makes it quite impossible to assert that Christ is the truth.

106

Such a counter on my part might be resisted. To argue as I have, it will be remarked, on the one hand, confuses religious questions with conceptual — if you will, epistemological — questions and, on the other, confuses the world-historical point of view with the agent's point of view — a point of view which has a genuine subjectivity and which recognises, as the world-historical point of view does not, that 'in morality and religion truth is a personal matter' (11). To contrast the world-historical point of view and the agent's point of view comes to contrasting the objective point of view which looks on, say, death as a medical and sociological fact and studies it in that manner, with the subjective point of view — the, if you will, existential point of view — in which one like Ivan Ilyitch asks about death in an entirely different manner, namely, what does the fact of death mean to me and what relevance does it have for the meaning of my life? Here such subjective thinking about death can reorient your whole attitude towards life and the point of your own life. Similarly, we can ask from the agent's point of view and in this existential manner: 'What is it for me to be a Christian?' or 'What is marriage really?' and we can ask these questions in a world-historical manner as when we ask about the history, development and variety of Christian doctrine or about the varieties of forms of marriage in the manner that a social scientist such as Westermarck would ask those questions. I do not want, as do many who utilise this distinction, to suggest the irrelevance of the world-historical point of view to the agent's point of view. But they are distinct points of view with different centres of interest, involving different language-games, which we play for different purposes.

Arguing as I have about the relevance of conceptual relativism, the counter-argument will continue, I have looked at things entirely from a world-historical perspective. The existing individual — the religious agent — is not interested in surveying all the forms of life, including all the religious forms of life. He is simply thoroughly caught up in a form of life and in that one form of life he is trying to make sense of his life. Similarly, and relatedly, I have confused, it will be argued, religious considerations with conceptual ones. In saying 'Christ is the truth and within Christ we find life', one makes a religious utterance. It is profoundly commissive for someone who avows it sincerely in a religious context. But it is not a piece of philosophy; it is not made from a world-historical point of view with those objective interests and it does not commit the believer to the world-historical claim that, independently of the language-game played, 'Christ is the truth' holds for all mankind. It is a remark that is made within a particular language-game for distinctively religious purposes. It has a profound point within those confines and from the existential point of view of a particular type of agent, but it makes no world-historical claim. It is not to be taken to hold or to have relevance outside of a particular language-game — a language-game which like all language-games is historically contingent.

I agree that it is a religious utterance and not a piece of philosophy and that it is conceptually at home when it is made from the agent's point of view. But I do not agree that it does not also make or try to make a world-historical claim. The agent thinks he is making a statement which not only holds for him and for people in his tribe but for all men as well, regardless of their condition (12). It is the key, so he believes, to their salvation. My point is that once he recognises the truth of conceptual relativism, he will also recognise that such utterances as 'Christ is the truth and the way' cannot be taken at their face value. (Perhaps I should say 'their apparent face value', for their obscurity hardly can make us confident of understanding what their face value is. But the point of speaking as I have above is that, for all their obscurity, they can hardly be taken as the mass of believers plainly wants to take them.) Whatever their real or depth grammar, they, if conceptual relativism is true, can never meet the Christian's religious expectations and aspirations once he clear-headedly accepts conceptual relativism, for, however else he takes them, as a religious agent he must take them as making universal claims which are incompatible with conceptual relativism.

I shall turn now to a second objection which it is natural to make to the case I am trying to make out, i.e. conceptual relativism supports scepticism about the claims of religion. How can the assertion that Christ is the truth be impossible since there are philosophically sophisticated individuals who

108

are conceptual relativists and who are committed to such an assertion? Since it is actual, how can it be impossible? Philosophers such as Holland, Malcolm and Phillips, philosophers committed to a Wittgensteinian form of conceptual relativism, assert — though hardly as a piece of philosophy — that Christ is the Truth. Moreover, to say that such assertions are irrational is to beg some central questions and to drag in some unspecified and problematic concept of irrationality. It is in effect to do little more than abuse the other position.

It is not so evident to me that such a claim on my part is unjustified or involves such evasiveness with 'irrationality'. In saying such behaviour is irrational, I am giving you to understand that if I have a system of belief p (in this case, Christianity) and I recognise that p can in the nature of the case have no greater claim to being true than the alternative systems of religious and/or ideological belief q, r, t, n, m, y, s, . . . , it is irrational for me to proclaim that p is the truth. Moreover, if p does not give warrant for claiming that there is something else about it, say that it answers in a profounder way than any of the alternative belief systems to fundamental human needs, then it cannot be rightly claimed of p that it ought to be accepted in preference to any of the other belief systems. But this is just the problem about belief systems that we must face if conceptual relativism is true. There are no grounds for Christianity or even theism having pride of place and in the very nature of the case there can — if conceptual relativism is true — be no such justification of a form of life. Mistakes and confusion can happen only vis-à-vis some particular argument or claim *within* a form of life and are detected by the employment of criteria distinctive of that form of life. But forms of life themselves cannot be appraised as such. Our very concepts settle for us the form of experience we have of the world. The thing to see — to use Winch's way of putting it — is 'that criteria of logic are not a direct gift of God, but arise out of, and are only intelligible in, the context of living or modes of social life as such' (13). Consequently — if conceptual relativism is true — one cannot correctly and intelligibly say of a whole mode of social life that it is either logical or illogical or rational or irrational. There is simply no way of appraising the practices themselves.

Those of us who engage in such discussions about belief system p (Christianity) operate out of similar linguistic frameworks and at least to some extent in operating with those languages share a common conception of rationality. Moreover, I agree with Winch that 'something can appear rational to someone only in terms of his understanding of what is and is not rational' (14). Now, given that and given our common understanding of rationality — a conception of rationality operative in many language-games which Westerners and no doubt most others as well ordinarily play — I appeal to that sense of 'rationality' in maintaining that it is irrational to make such an assertion about truth as that expounded in the previous paragraph in the face of such an understanding of alternatives. That is, as we use 'rational', such a position is plainly irrational.

There is a further thing to be noted here. Such Wittgensteinian fideists (Holland, Malcolm, Phillips) in varying degrees transform their conception of religious belief in the face of such problems. Phillips talks of 'subjective truth' vis-à-vis religion and for him to talk of God seems to be a way of talking in a culturally determinate way of agapeistic love (15). Malcolm takes it to be the case that to *believe that* God exists is to believe something utterly problematic, e.g. to believe something of doubtful intelligibility, though to *believe in* God is quite unproblematic (16). It begins to appear that they unwittingly have created a new or at least a radically altered language-game with Christian terms and an atheistic substance.

If religious truth is 'subjective truth', then indeed there is no conflict between accepting belief system p (Christianity) as embodying the claim Christ is the truth and acknowledging that systems q, r, t, n, m, y, s, . . . , are equally legitimate forms of life. Which one one is to accept for oneself is simply a matter of what language-game one happens to have learned to play and what one is willing to commit oneself to. Genetically, the former is culturally determined and epistemologically it is, as Phillips puts it, basically a personal matter (17). There is no conflict given such a construal between these alternative belief systems, but there is also a very considerable transformation of Christian-talk and belief. 'Christ is the truth' comes to have a very different feel and, as

110

Wisdom points out, there is a loss of something and indeed a loss of something which seems to be of the essence of religion (18).

What I am maintaining is that if we take very seriously such relativity — that is, if we really take what is involved in such conceptions to heart — we will end up either as sceptics, Quixotic knights of faith committed to what in our own terms is plainly irrational, or reductionists committed to a form of belief that is so transformed that it is in substance atheistic. The latter is itself a thinly disguised form of scepticism. So it seems to me that the acceptance of such a philosophical framework as I have described in this chapter can only lead, where thought through vigorously, to a form of scepticism, since it is a plain implication in our discourse that if p is irrational then p ought not to be believed. Wittgensteinian fideism, when pressed, leads or should lead to religious scepticism.

6 On Dining with the Theologian

I

In the previous chapter I uncritically accepted the basic philosophical claims of what I have called conceptual relativism and by working with them I tried to show that if conceptual relativism is true, then one ought to be a religious sceptic. That is, if one is convinced of the truth of conceptual relativism, one should adopt a sceptical attitude towards religion rather than a fideistic or neutral attitude. Elsewhere I have subjected conceptual relativism to a detailed critique and I by no means wish to leave the impression that I have changed my mind about this (1). I am firmly convinced that such forms of relativism, particularly those which take a Wittgensteinian turn, are one of the most significant developments in philosophy, but I also think that the key concepts in it and in the other forms of conceptual relativism I worked with in Chapter 5 are too impressionistically conceived and too unclearly delineated to justify the startling conclusions drawn from them. In particular, I think that concepts such as forms of life, forms of language, language-games, mode of discourse, universe of discourse, self-contained discourse, linguistic framework or conceptual framework are all too problematic — too indeterminate — even to begin to bear the conceptual weight that is put on them.

Wittgensteinian conceptual relativists would have us believe that what is given are the forms of life and that the forms of language are the forms of life. Each form of life contains its own distinctive criteria for intelligibility, rationality and truth; each is all right as it is in the sense that there can be no *overall* conceptual difficulties connected with it appropriately assessable by some external criterion. But until what is to count as 'a form of language' or 'a form of life' is stated and elucidated in a far more careful and explicit way than the way it has been stated and elucidated, no such extensive and remarkable conceptual claims can safely be made on the basis of the doctrine that the forms of language are the forms of life and that what is given are the forms of life. Like the so-called Whorf-Sapir hypothesis, it is suggestive and indeed even disturbing, but nothing definite and soundly founded can be built on it as it stands. Working with the cenceptual tools and arguments conceptual relativists have given us, we can have no well-founded idea whether it is true or false or even very reasonable to claim that there can be no overall conceptual difficulties in a form of life or that each form of life has its own distinctive criteria of intelligibility and truth.

It seems counter-intuitive to claim that there can be no overall conceptual difficulties in Christian Science, but perhaps that peculiar brand of Christianity would not be said to be a form of life? Perhaps it is Christianity or perhaps even just religion which is a form of life? But with the bare concept of religion we have something fairly rarefied, and when we come to actual historical forms of Christianity it again seems counter-intuitive to say that they can be in no overall conceptual difficulties and that they can only be appraised from within. Moreover, in this connection, it should be remembered that no convincing argument has ever been given as to why it is impossible relevantly to assess social practices and forms of life as such or why it is not the business of a philosophy to criticise and assess forms of life and *Weltanschauungen*. The fundamental concepts involved here are far too indeterminate and problematic to sustain the sweeping conclusions of the conceptual relativists.

All the same, conceptual relativism remains highly suggestive and sufficiently conceptually nagging to be a fundamental centre of philosophical interest. It is not inconceivable that in some more carefully delineated form it will come to be seen as the most plausible conceptual rock bottom in philosophy.

Be that as it may, I have not been concerned in this book with its attempted refutation or defence, but only to show that from what can be made of conceptual relativism as it stands, scepticism concerning the claims of the Judaic-Christian religion, rather than fideism or neutralism, is the natural and indeed reasonable conclusion to draw from such a philosophical position. (I have assumed in discussing it that it actually can be coherently formulated. This very assumption might usefully be challenged in spite of the intuitive attractiveness of conceptual relativism.)

II

Hitherto with both the empiricist critiques of religion and with the critique I have drawn from conceptual relativism, I have been concerned with critiques of religion relying on general conceptions about what it makes sense to say. Much contemporary analytical work in the philosophy of religion has abandoned any attempt to find a general meaning criterion in virtue of which the putative truth-claims of religion can be shown to be unintelligible or incoherent and has gone instead into the detail of actual theological argument in an attempt to establish the actual incoherence or at least the baselessness of religious and theological claims. J. N. Findlay's celebrated 'Can God's Existence Be Disproved'?, Paul Edwards's 'Difficulties in the Idea of God', B. A. Farrell's 'Psychological Theory and the Belief in God', Ronald Hepburn's unfortunately neglected 'Poetry and Religious Belief' and his 'Christianity and Paradox', C. B. Martin's 'Religious Belief', W. I. Matson's 'The Existence of God', Antony Flew's 'God and Philosophy', and my own 'In Defense of Atheism' and 'The Quest for God' are cases in point (2). An effort is made in most of this work to dine with the theologians and to examine their arguments in detail and/or to examine the fundamental concepts of religion internally. Such critiques attempt to exhibit from within extensive defects in religious concepts — defects of such a magnitude as to make religious belief or at least Jewish and Christian belief untenable. The drive is, as Hepburn puts it, to engage in a 'painstaking examination and re-examination of problems in the entire field of apologetics', eschewing reliance on any 'decisive verification-test' or 'solemn Declaration of Meaninglessness' (3). A recurrent counter from their critics, however, is that their detailed arguments implicitly presuppose the kind of empiricist conceptions of meaning we have already examined.

114

The range of topics covered — from necessary existence to Christology and ethics — is so wide that any attempt to summarise it here would at best produce the skeletons of significant arguments and counter-arguments. What I shall do is take three representative and central arguments and examine their force.

Ronald Hepburn in 'Christianity and Paradox' and in 'From World to God', Antony Flew in 'God and Philosophy' (chap. ii), and Paul Edwards in 'Difficulties in the Idea of God', have argued for the incoherence of a central concept of God embedded in the Jewish-Christian tradition. In the Book of Common Prayer, we are told that 'There is but one living and true God, everlasting, without body, parts, or passions; of infinite power, wisdom, and goodness, the Maker and Preserver of all things both visible and invisible'. This is not all a Christian or Jew is talking about when he speaks of God, but, it would for a very large number of them at least, be an essential part of what they are talking about. This core conception has been put in capsule form by Flew as follows: to speak of God is to speak of 'a Being which is unique, unitary, incorporeal, infinitely powerful, wise and good, personal without passions, and the maker and preserver of the universe'. These critics of religion maintain that this conception of God, of central importance in Judaism and Christianity, is incoherent. But if a concept is incoherent, one ought not, even as an article of faith, to take it on trust that the concept in question has application. If the concept of God is actually incoherent (not that we just mistakenly think that it is), we have decisive grounds for not believing in God, and thus Christian and Jewish theology and their respective faiths as well would be utterly undermined by a line of philosophical reasoning.

So it is of considerable moment to try to determine whether this important concept of God is incoherent. Some of the central reasons given for making the claim that it is incoherent are that when 'God' occurs in a biblical sentence such as 'But God showed his love for us in that when we were yet sinners Christ died for us', (a) God is not identifiable, (b) it is senseless to maintain such a being can love or fail to love, and (c) there is operating here a sense of 'Creator' which is self-contradictory. In arguing for (a), Hepburn and Flew

115

point out that God is taken to be an incorporeal individual who is not taken to be a part of the universe, but, as maker and preserver of the universe, the whole universe is said to be dependent upon him. The problem, however, is: We have no idea at all how to identify, pick out, a Being so characterised. We have no way of knowing whether or not such a concept has or could have an actual application. It may well be, as the ontological argument should in effect make us aware, that such a concept must always have an application or never have application. Yet we still need to know whether it does or even could have application. Unless there is some way in principle at least of deciding this, no question about either the existence or non-existence of such a God can arise (4). God is held to be an individual, albeit incorporeal, i.e. purely spiritual, but we have no idea of what counts as an incorporeal thing, a purely spiritual agent, a non-physical agent, an unlimited agent, and the like. The latter putative characteristic would seem to preclude any picking out or identification, but even if we can put aside that consideration and admit the uniqueness of God — his radical difference from dependent creation — he must be at least in principle in some way identifiable, if we are to have any understanding of what we are talking about. But there is no understanding of what it would be like to identify such a putative individual. We have no idea of what, now or hereafter, we would have to encounter to encounter God or an infinite individual. Yet an individual which in principle is not identifiable is a contradiction in terms and if we have no idea what even in principle or in theory it would be like to identify such an alleged individual, then the concept of such an individual is so problematic as to be incoherent. But Hepburn and Flew maintain that this is the difficulty we are in about God.

The second point is also forcefully argued. Edwards points out that we can conceive of a loving God with a body, but by contrast an incorporeal, utterly spiritual reality loving or failing to love is a very problematic notion indeed. While rejecting logical behaviourism — psychological predicates cannot be defined in behaviouristic terms — Edwards argues in a standard Wittgensteinian fashion that 'psychological predicates are *logically* tied to the behaviour of organisms' (5). He is not claiming that a person is just his body but that

116

'however much more than a body a human being may be, one cannot sensibly talk about this "more" without presupposing (as part of what one means, and not as a mere contingent fact) that he is a living organism' (6). God by definition is alleged to be without any local existence or bodily presence. But what would it be like for an x to be just loving without doing anything or being capable of doing anything? One is at a loss here. And what would it be like for an x to act in a loving manner without behaving in a certain way? Surely no sense is attached to 'acting lovingly but not doing anything' and surely 'to do something', 'to behave in a certain way', is to make — though this is not all that it is — certain bodily movements. And it would not make sense to say that x moves y if it in turn made no sense to say that x either could or could not act in a certain way. But for it to make sense to speak of x's acting or failing to act, x must have a body. Thus if 'love' is to continue to mean anything at all near to what it normally means, it is meaningless to say that God loves mankind. Similar considerations apply to the other psychological predicates tied to the concept of God. Such considerations about these predicates give us further evidence for believing that the concept of God is incoherent.

Flew also argues that there is an internal inconsistency in the very concept of God, for a God whose will can be disobeyed cannot (logically cannot) be regarded as the sovereign creator (sustainer) of his creation. Yet the very concept of God in the Judaeo-Christian form of life requires both that God be a sovereign creator and that God can be disobeyed. It is not to the point, Flew argues, to reply that there is nothing incoherent here, for God in making us free moral agents — a quality essential to our being agents — of logical necessity had to give us power to flout his wishes; for God not only created us in the sense of having made us but also created us in the sense that he is the constant and essential sustaining cause of everything within the universe. The concept of creator, when applied to God, is such that 'absolutely nothing happens save by his ultimate undetermined determination with his consenting ontological support' (7). But then there is no possibility of disobeying God, for 'as Creator he could not decide simply to leave to their own devices creatures already autonomously existing.

He both designs and makes them in full knowledge and determination of what they will ever do or fail to do . . . If creation is in, autonomy is out' (8).

Hepburn, Flew and Edwards employ such arguments to establish the incoherence of this very central concept of God. Others have vigorously argued that their efforts fail. Williams, for example, argues that the soundness of Flew's last argument depends on the correctness of the quite questionable assumption that to say God is the cause of every event in the universe is to say that some fact about God's will is the *sufficient* condition for the taking place of each and every event in the universe. But Williams points out that all the Jew or Christian need maintain is that 'for every event there is some fact about God's will which is its necessary condition'. However, 'to say this is to *say* no more than that nothing happens without God's at least permitting it to happen; and there is nothing incoherent in the notion of someone's permitting himself to be disobeyed' (9).

The other two arguments directed to exhibiting the incoherence of the concept of God have also been forcefully criticised. Here two things must be looked for: (a) particular defects in the above arguments, and (b) the extent to which (if at all) their soundness presupposes the soundness of the verificationist arguments we considered in previous chapters. Evans and MacIntyre, for example, argue that these arguments presuppose what they regard as empiricist dogmas while their proponents believe they stand independently of the correctness of such verificationist arguments (10).

My strategy will be to lay out and then examine specific criticisms of the above arguments that the concept of God is incoherent. I shall be concerned to assess the soundness of the argument that the concept of God is incoherent because God is not — where 'God' is used non-anthropomorphically — identifiable and the argument that 'a loving disembodied spirit' is a senseless collocation of words. Flew's further argument that 'Creator', when applied to God, gives us an incoherent conception seems to me, for the reasons Williams gives, less likely to be secure than the other arguments, and I shall not consider it.

I shall start by considering the arguments against the conceptual claim that it is senseless to say, as Christians do, that God loves mankind or that God is infinitely loving. Edwards and Flew maintain that such religious talk is unintelligible, for an x could love only if that x could do something or fail to do something, i.e. if that x could act. But that an x can act presupposes that x has a body.

Properly to assess criticisms of this claim, we first need to have its grounds more clearly before us. When we say 'God is loving' or 'God is infinitely loving', we imply that God can act, that God can do certain things; that is, that God is an agent. It is by now evident that to talk of someone's doing something is not just to talk of the occurrence of certain bodily movements. Yet it would still seem to be the case that to say 'x did y' or 'x could do y' entails 'x has a body'. We have no idea of what it could mean to say that someone was loving without his being an agent who could do certain things. And to be able to act, indeed to be an agent, is — though this is not all that it is — to have a body. (Even in the secondary and doubtfully relevant use 'chemical agent', there is still something with a spatio-temporal location.) But God is said to be a pure spirit, a bodiless spirit and an infinite individual transcendent to the world and completely without any spatio-temporal location. He does not even have the 'subtle rarefied body' ascribed to ghosts and poltergeists. He indeed has a name but no local habitation. Thus it makes no sense to say of such a putative reality that it is infinitely loving or even loving.

Such an argument does not require or presuppose the verifiability criterion but turns on the meanings of the terms 'loving', 'agent', 'action', 'doing something', 'being non-spatio-temporal', and 'having no body'. The claim is that when we carefully reflect on the actual structure of our language, i.e. the depth grammar of the language, we will come to see that 'disembodied love' or 'bodiless action' like '3 a.m. on Mars' or 'wife without husband' is an unintelligible collocation of words. This claim rests on no general theory of language; it is no more dependent on neo-behaviourist or materialist conceptions than on verificationist ones. Rather, it turns on the kind of understanding we should gain by careful attention to our actual use of words in a particular area,

Donald Evans and W. D. Hudson have tried to counter such arguments and establish that these alleged conceptual connections do not abtain and that the 'concept of an agent without a body is intelligible' (11). Reflect on this analogy. In our actual experience we have never found smoke without fire, but this does not at all establish that we cannot conceive of there being smoke without fire. Similarly, 'although, in our experience of human agents, agency does not occur without movement of the agent's body, and though we may be unable to imagine what it would be like to be an agent without a body, nevertheless' an 'agent without a body is not inconceivable'. We must not confuse what is consistently thinkable — conceivable (logically possible) — with what is imaginable. I cannot imagine what a million-sided diamond would look like, but such a figure is plainly consistently thinkable. Once we reflect on this distinction and apply it to God-talk, it would seem to be the case that it is not unintelligible to speak of 'God as an agent without a body, even though we cannot imagine what it must be like to be God' (13).

Surely there is this distinction between what is imaginable and what is consistently thinkable. But the point is that Edwards and Flew are not just claiming that they cannot imagine an agent without a body but 'that talk about a disembodied consciousness is unintelligible' (14). In arguing about what is and what is not unintelligible, are we reduced, or finally reduced, to a confessional state wherein Edwards and Flew could only say they have not the 'slightest idea of what is meant' by such talk, while Hudson and Evans could in turn only reply that they by contrast have some idea of what is meant? Hudson tries to establish that this is not our situation by providing us with reasons for thinking that fluent speakers of the language — believers and non-believers alike — can and do understand what is meant by 'disembodied consciousness' and 'an infinitely loving bodiless agent'.

Hudson first points out that in thinking about human

agency, we need to distinguish between the agent and his situation. The agent 'is logically distinct from his situation. We can ask him what he is going to do about his situation' (15). A judge takes bribes and he is found out and disgraced. His life with his family and in the small town in which he lives subsequently becomes intolerable and he takes to drink and comes to have high blood-pressure and ulcers. His conviction, disgrace, conflict with family and neighbours, his drinking and resultant high blood-pressure and ulcers all can be described as aspects of his situation. We can distinguish between him and his situation and we can ask him what he is going to do about his situation, e.g. about his family circumstances or high blood-pressure. However, in considering something like his situation's being intolerable, his being disgraced or his having high blood-pressure, we have matters that, according to Hudson, are aspects of his situation. But the judge's having high blood-pressure or finding the situation intolerable is also something that is 'in' his 'body or mind, whereas the disgrace is not', though 'they are both aspects of his situation' (16). The recognition of this is, for Hudson, philosophically crucial, for he goes on to say that this shows that in contexts such as the one just described, there is no sharp line to be drawn between the judge's body and the rest of his situation. But the judge — the agent — is logically distinct from his situation even though in such contexts his body is part of his situation. From this it follows that since his situation is logically distinct from him, so his body is too. He, as agent, 'is systematically illusive to both. He is, therefore, an agent, not logically identifiable with his body' (17). His body may 'legitimately be thought of as a part of his situation' and, as agent, he is logically distinct from his situation, and thus we can conclude 'that the concept of an agent without a body is intelligible' (18). And if this is so, 'bodiless action' and 'disembodied love' can also be seen to be intelligible, though indeed strange.

There are, however, crippling difficulties in the notion that an agent's body 'may legitimately be thought of as a part of his situation' (19). Why not, let us ask, draw a sharp line, i.e. make a conceptual distinction, between one's body and one's situation? This is part of the reason we have such concepts in the first place, and dictionaries in defining 'situation' make

121

the contrast quite unselfconsciously in speaking of 'the position in which one finds oneself'. The answer Hudson gives is that certain aspects of his body are or can be parts of his situation and we must not identify 'being an agent' with 'having a live body of such and such complexity'. The judge's having high blood-pressure or a person's having aggressive tendencies or being a kleptomaniac can be an aspect of his body and at the same time also an aspect of his situation. 'Aspect of his body' is odd here. It certainly does not mean 'part'; rather, it amplifies in such a context into 'something that is going on in his body', e.g. high blood-pressure, or 'something that he *has*', e.g. aggressive tendencies or kleptomania. But the point is that what is properly ascribable to his body is also characterisable as aspects of his situation.

There are things which are distinguishable but not separable. We conceptually distinguish between equilateral triangles and equiangular triangles and yet all equilateral triangles must be equiangular and all equiangular triangles must be equilateral. Similarly, there could be things one has or one is, such as being a kleptomaniac, which perforce are also in certain contexts part of one's situation. That is, they are a part of one's circumstances in an account which is made of one. But surely there is a distinction between, on the one hand, a man's body and what is going on in his body and, on the other hand, his circumstances or situation. That his wife nags, that his daughter leaves home, that he is dismissed are aspects of his situation. They are not happenings in his body. That he has high blood-pressure or an ulcer is something that is a happening in his body. That he is a kleptomaniac or is agressive is something, unlike his wife's nagging, which is a behaviour trait of his own.

Yet things are not so simple and Hudson's remarks are not idle, for, viewed from a certain perspective, the judge's high blood-pressure and his kleptomania are part of his circumstances. In sizing up his situation, they would have to be taken into consideration. But one, say a physiologist, might not want to consider his circumstances or situation at all, but only want to consider what was going on in him and happening to his body and he certainly could and naturally would so regard his high blood-pressure or kleptomania. We can always distinguish between talk of his body and talk of his situation.

122

However, even if the above argument is somehow mistaken, and there is no clear distinction to be drawn between a man's body and his situation, this does not give us sufficient reason to think that the agent can be distinguished from both his body and the rest of his situation and to infer that the concept of a human agent without a body is intelligible. Why not simply say instead that some aspects of the agent's situation are logically distinct from him, e.g. his wife's nagging, and some are not, e.g. his kleptomania or finding his situation intolerable? If my argument in the previous paragraph is near to the mark, such talk is at least strained — as it indeed seems to be — but if we are to follow out Hudson's line of reasoning about having kleptomania being both 'in' one and also being an aspect of one's situation, it is more natural to speak, given such assumptions, of some aspects of the agent's situation's being distinct from him and some not. But to try to talk of him as if he were distinct from his body is not at all the natural thing to say here. It is certainly not a conclusion we must draw or a conceptualisation we must make given the belief that some bodily happenings are also aspects of one's situation. Given this and given the antecedent problematic nature of 'a bodiless agent', Hudson's conclusion is not warranted.

No sense has been given to a human agent's not being an aspect of a situation when his body is an aspect of that situation. Wherever (if ever) it is even remotely plausible to say that his body is an aspect of his situation, it is also plausible to say that he is not distinguishable from his situation. To the extent that this causes conceptual disquietude — as I believe it should — the notion of his body's being an aspect of his situation should also arouse our suspicions. (Hudson's use of quotation marks around 'in' and the qualifier 'so to say' in his 'the kleptomania is, so to say, "in" Smith's body . . . ' is a giveaway) (20).

One could, as Edwards does, and as I do, agree with Hudson that an agent is not logically identifiable with his body — assuming that this is taken to mean that 'I am my body', 'Jones is his body', or 'An agent is his body' are not like genuine logical identities, e.g. 'A father is a male parent' or 'A puppy is a young dog' — and still deny that 'disembodied agency' is an intelligible notion. Rather, as we

123

have seen, Edwards' argument is that 'psychological predicates are logically tied to the behaviour of organisms' and not that 'a person is just his body, that there are no private experiences or that feelings are simply ways of behaving'. The claim is that, whatever else a person or agent is besides being a body, one cannot intelligibly talk of this 'more' 'without presupposing (as part of what one means and not as a mere contingent fact) that he is a living organism'. Given the language-games we play, 'a wife has a husband' and 'a forest has trees' are conceptual remarks which do not claim logical identity and are quite different from contingent statements such as 'a human being has a liver' or 'a dog has some hair'. 'Wherever there is a human agent there is a body' is not like 'Wherever there is smoke there is fire', but like 'Wherever there is a triangle there is a three-sided figure'. The agent or the 'I' may be systematically illusive and not capable of being fully described in behaviourial terms, but this does not at all show or even suggest what it could *mean* to speak of a bodiless person, self or agent.

Thus talk of human beings will not provide a model for speaking intelligibly, as we must, of God's being a transcendent disembodied agent. Hudson — but not Evans — grants that we should not, as some Christians do, speak of God as a person, for persons must, Hudson agrees, have bodies, but we can still speak of God as an agent. But Hudson has not shown how we can sensibly speak of a human agent without a body or conceive of anything analogous to human agency, which might be said to love or care, without presupposing, as part of what one *means*, that this agent has a body. It is not that I doubt that agency can in fact occur in the absence of bodily movement, but that I doubt the intelligibility of the sentence — and not simply on verificationist grounds — 'Agency can occur in the absence of bodily movements'. It may well be the case that we can always ask as agent 'What is he doing or going to do about his situation?' but this does not at all show that 'an agent is systematically elusive to his body' if, by this obscure phrase, we mean that he need not have a body to exist.

In contrast to Hudson, Evans, I believe, would counter that my confidence here springs from sticking to human agency as our model for God's agency and failing to consider other cases in which we can and do quite intelligibly speak of bodiless agents. Whether there are any such agents is another matter, but our talk here, Evans believes, is not unintelligible. Where the bodiless agent is a poltergeist, for example, and where

> what is observed has considerable similarity to the results of familiar human actions, we can meaningfully apply predicates which normally apply to human beings. Whether or not there are poltergeists, I do not know. But I have no trouble in understanding talk about them: for example, 'The poltergeist got angry'. This statement is not exhaustively analyzed in terms of observables such as flying cutlery, nor do I need to picture, surreptitiously, an embodied consciousness in order to understand what is being said. It is true that we learn to use predicates as 'angry' in relation to bodily behaviour, but this does not mean that talk about bodiless consciousness is unintelligible (21).

But the very bodilessness of ghosts and poltergeists is in question. Hudson, unlike Evans, dismisses such examples on the ground that they are taken to 'have "bodies" of a sort' and Geach, rather derisively, in such contexts, speaks of 'ethereal bodies' and 'subtle bodies' (22). But whatever we have going for us here, we do not have a clear case of a bodiless agent. In reply to Evans, Edwards remarks, appropriately enough, that when someone says 'the poltergeist is angry' we can well take him, on the one hand, to be talking of a small, shadowy human-like being — something that might even be photographed or in some other way be detected by sophisticated physical instruments — or, on the other hand, to be saying that certain strange things are going on and that we do not know what causes them' (23). In both cases, such talk 'is intelligible but it throws no light whatever on the meaning of statements about disembodied spirits' (24). But if, by contrast, we try to conceive of a poltergeist as a pure spirit who works his tricks without a body, all the old difficulties about understanding re-emerge. Evans can only be as confident as he is that poltergeist-talk is intelligible because he does not distinguish between these different ways of construing such talk. Both God-talk and poltergeist-talk are plainly intelligible though indeed superstitious *if* the objects of that discourse are taken to have a body or if the key terms in this discourse function as umbrella terms standing for mysterious and unexplained natural phenomena. But as Judaeo-Christian discourse has developed, something more than that has been attempted. But 'the more' that has been tried to be said is generally acknowledged to be problematical. The argument we have been considering gives us good grounds for believing that 'God is our loving heavenly Father' or 'God's acts' are, where 'God' is construed non-anthropomorphically, so problematical as to be unintelligible.

However, the idea of a bodiless agent or pure spirit dies hard. It is part of an ancient Platonic or Cartesian way of conceptualising which can easily become a captivating image. Starting with the plain fact that we have private experiences — that we have pains we do not show, wishes we hide and anxieties and feelings of love we do not reveal — it is easy to be led into accepting a picture of human nature in which our make-up includes, besides our bodies, a wholly immaterial thing, our minds or souls. It is this which thinks and feels. It is this which loves; it is this that is central to agency; that love is shown in action or bodily behaviour is not essential. Rather, love or thought itself is essentially a mental act of an agent who may or may not have a body. 'Love', like other mental terms, stands for a private experience.

Indeed, we come to understand how to use this term when embodied agents act in certain distinctive ways and we would not regard it as appropriate to use it if they acted in other ways. But, as we gain mastery of it, we come to realise that it denotes not just distinctive ranges of behaviour, but certain private experiences that we all have as well. Each of us knows what these private experiences are like from his own case, i.e. from having the experiences. In saying that God or any disembodied being loves, we say that this being has the same or similar feelings — the same or similar private experiences — as those we have when we feel love for someone. Whether the having of such an experience does or even can result in distinctive actions is not essential to give meaning to the concept of loving, though indeed we would never have come

126

to use the word in the first place if there were no characteristic modes of behaviour that go with the proper application of that term. But it does not only have meaning in such a behavioural context.

Ryle, Wittgenstein, Geach and many others have utilised profound philosophical talents to break the spell of this picture of the mind without falling into the behaviourist trap of denying that there is private experience. The arguments utilised by me and directed to establishing the incoherence of applying the predicate 'loving' to God were in this tradition. We should remind ourselves, in reflecting on the central issues here, that God is conceived of as being without passions and that even Aquinas thought disembodied spirits could only think and will but that they were without feelings. He did not have God in mind, but surely similar considerations seem at least to apply to him. Where God is not conceived utterly anthropomorphically, what does it *mean* to say he has feelings? Well, it means that he has the same or a very similar experience to that I have when I love disinterestedly or feel concern. But to say this will not help. It is like saying, Wittgenstein points out, 'I know what it means to say "It is 3 a.m. on the moon". It is to say that it is the same time on the moon as it is when it is correctly said in Cambridge "It is 3 a.m.".' But it is just the idea of its being any time at all on the moon that is at issue. If I say I caught the same kind of fish you did, we can take our fish out of our creels and compare. If I say that I have the same kind of headache you do, we can compare mental notes by describing our headaches more fully and our behaviour can be carefully observed. There are checks for both claims but there is no check on the alleged truth-claim 'God loves mankind'. (Here, note, in defending our contention, a verificationist note enters. Whether it is necessary that it be appealed to here, I do not know.) We understand the term 'love' when applied to human beings. Walt Disneywise, we can extend it, with increasing uneasiness, to chimps, monkeys, dogs, cats and pet skunks. But it is utterly indeterminate when applied to birds, snakes or frogs. To say 'Fred has a collection of loving earthworms' or 'That sparrow can feel love' is utterly without truth-value. To understand talk of love, we must understand it against a rather distinctive behavioural background.

127

Attaching sense to an expression is not to be indentified with any private experience that accompanies that expression. Words have meaning only if they have a role in the language. If someone has a certain experience on hearing or seeing a word, this does not establish that he understands it or that it is intelligible. What is necessary — I do not say sufficient — for its being intelligible is that it has a role in the language and that he and others can get into a way of using these expressions. 'Love', like other mental words, is used only in association with a host of behavioural terms and terms relating to physical characteristics. Take away such a background and we have no understanding of utterances in which 'love' and 'loving' occur. 'An immaterial, incorporeal spirit loves', 'Pure spirit is loving', 'There is a non-spatio-temporal reality which is infinitely loving' are thus unintelligible and we therefore have good grounds for thinking the Judaeo-Christian concept of God is an incoherent concept.

IV

I shall now turn to the argument that the concept of God is incoherent because 'God' is a term which allegedly functions referentially and yet 'God', when employed non-anthropomorphically, does not denote a reality which even in principle can be identified.

To see more clearly what is at issue, let us start by following Flew's methodological advice and ask straight off '*What is this God* that Christians and Jews speak of?' Here, Flew remarks, we are asking in an external way a question 'from right outside the system' (25). But unless we put it like this 'in this external way some fundamental questions will go unasked' (26). At issue here is whether the putative referring expression 'God' actually applies to anything (27). Recall that the God of the Judaeo-Christian tradition is said to be an 'individual, yet everything else is dependent on him, infinite, though no part of the universe, but still transcendent to the universe while at the same time remaining the saviour and redeemer of all men'. Given these very extraordinary defining characteristics, extraordinarily conjoined, there is, as Flew points out, no escaping the question: 'How could we identify

128

the Being so specified?' How could we, for example, identify an absolutely independent being? Given such a response to the question 'What is this God?' the question of identification becomes acute. 'Until and unless', Flew continues, 'this can be answered, there can be no question of existence or of non-existence: because there has been no proper account of what it would be for him to be or not to be; of what, in short, he would be' (28).

As we have seen, many terms, e.g. 'justice', 'credible', 'choice', 'space', are perfectly intelligible but do not refer to corporeal things. But, as Flew rightly points out, they do not refer or even purport to refer to incorporeal things either. Yet 'God' by contrast is a putative referring expression and the question of how, if at all, we can identify its referent is immediately relevant. Moreover, 'God', unlike 'justice', is a word purportedly standing — given the Judaeo-Christian characterisation of 'God' — for an extraordinary individual. But then the problem of how it would be possible to identify this alleged individual becomes acute. The 'fact that people, whether in the Bible or elsewhere, employ a term intending it to refer to a certain (sort of) object is not enough to show that the intended reference is or could be achieved' (29). 'Does or could' Flew asks, 'the word "God" "have application" or "apply to any actual object"?' (30).

To say 'God' is not a label for a corporeal thing but an incorporeal thing or reality is to say something that squares with our actual use of God-talk, but is all the same completely unhelpful, for 'incorporeal thing' or 'incorporeal reality' is not itself 'an expression for a known and certainly identifiable sort of being . . . ' (31). The same questions arise about the possible identification of a referent for these expressions that caused the trouble about 'God' in the first place. The phrases 'incorporeal thing', 'incorporeal reality' or 'incorporeal substance' at best tell us only that what we are talking about is not corporeal, but they do not tell us what is being referred to or indicate how we could in any way gain any positive understanding of what is being talked about. The characterisation is negative and has the difficulties of the *via negativa*. 'God' indeed is supposed to refer to an utterly unique reality, but, utterly unique or not, it still remains the case that since 'God' allegedly stands for an infinite, non-spatio-temporal individual, 'he has to be at least in principle identifiable in some way' (32). But the rub is that we have no idea how to make such an identification.

It does not help to say with Aquinas that 'God is called being as being entity itself' or with Tillich that 'God is being itself not a being' or that 'God is the foundation of being' or that 'God is the world-ground', for we have no more idea what would or logically could count as an identification of what is allegedly referred to by 'entity itself', 'being-itself', 'foundation of being', 'world-ground' than we do of 'God' or 'incorporeal being', and with our above *supposed* elucidations of 'God' we do not even have phrases which have a use — and thus some kind of meaning — by being a part of a stream of life.

Putting aside such obscure talk of 'Being-itself', 'world-ground' and the like, it will be replied that Flew, and Hepburn as well, have misconstrued God-talk and are looking for the identification of 'God' in the wrong way. For the sake of the argument of this chapter we have put aside relying on verificationist arguments, but, it has been replied, the arguments we have used in this section essentially do rest — albeit surreptitiously — on verificationist arguments, for what they are implicitly requiring for identification of the referent of a referring expression in general and for 'God' in particular is that what is referred to be in some way, directly or indirectly, empirically identifiable. But, of course, that which is transcendent to the world and non-spatio-temporal cannot be so identified. Flew betrays his unargued and indeed unacknowledged verificationist assumptions when in a crucial passage he takes it as absolutely essential to ascertain whether the key word 'God' 'does or could *apply to any actual object*' (33). Flew, it is natural to reply, is still refuting again the anthropomorphism devastatingly criticised by Hume. But, of course, 'God' — where we are not being anthropomorphites — does not and could not apply to an actual object. That would make God into an existent among existents, albeit an extraordinary existent. But whatever God is, he is not any kind of existent or object at all. The kind of reality applicable to God is of a radically different order and anyone who has a proper understanding of the concept of God in the religious stream of life would realise that, and consequently

130

no question of such an empirical identification of God could possibly arise. God must be identified conceptually.

Such a rejoinder appears to be fair enough. But given the radical difference in the alleged kind of reality in question, Flew and Hepburn are surely justified in asking for a bill of particulars, including some elucidation of what is meant by the at least apparently problematic notion 'conceptual identification'. Given our garden variety notions of identification, no identification of 'God' seems possible and yet 'God' is supposed to be a label for an infinite, absolutely independent individual and thus, in some way, some identification and specification of referent should be possible. After all, what could it mean to say that x is an individual yet that it is logically impossible to identify x?

It is not enough by way of reply simply to say 'God is other' or a radically different kind of reality, though indeed it is understandable that it would be maintained that, in trying to come to understand the kind of reality which is involved, we must firmly put aside, as Wisdom has so persistently tried to get us to put aside, the idea that in some obscure way religious beliefs are experimental hypotheses about the world. Trying to understand the concept of God in these terms has, it is argued, shipwrecked our philosophical understanding of the concept of God. We must, if we would understand God-talk, put aside our implicitly unitary and empiricist conceptions of 'what is so' and 'the facts'.

It is, as Phillips puts it, as senseless to say 'God's existence is not a fact' as it is to say 'God's existence is a fact' (34). We need carefully to consider the question 'What *kind* of reality is divine reality?' We should compare this question not with 'Is this physical object real or not?' but with the different question 'What kind of reality is the reality of physical objects?' To ask 'Is God real?' is analogous to asking 'Are physical objects real?' rather than to asking 'Is the abominable snowman real?' The former two questions are not to be answered by carrying out an investigation, and for someone who understands what he is saying there can be no question of an *empirical* or *experiential* identification of what we are talking about when we are talking about 'God' or 'physical object'. We must come to understand that in both cases we are not asking questions about the reality of

131

this or that. We are not asking questions about the reality of some matter of fact. To so conceive of God is to commit the category mistake of conceiving of God as a reality within the conceptual framework of the reality of the physical world. But in speaking of God we are speaking of an utterly different kind of reality. God belongs to a category by himself to which no other reality belongs.

We come to learn the kind of reality God is by coming to understand a theistic religious tradition such as Judaism or Christianity. As children we learn to identify God, and slowly gain a sense of his reality, by learning stories and observing religious practices. It is in this context that as children we form an idea of God. As adults — indeed, even as theologians — we only deepen and extend these ideas that come to us in religious stories and services.

In speaking of this God of developed religious traditions, we are speaking of a conception of reality which is said to have necessary existence. A god who could begin to exist or cease to exist is not the God of developed Judaeo-Christianity. Unlike my reality or the reality of my pencil or even the reality of the everlasting stars, what we call 'God' is said to be non-contingent and necessary. He exists in a quite timeless manner; we cannot even rightly speak of him as having endless duration. To say this need not be to say what is very likely an incoherency, namely that God is a logically necessary being. God's necessity and non-contingency could be much more plausibly otherwise construed, and construed in such a way as to make evident how God's reality is conceived to be *sui generis*. Plantinga does this with economy and force and I shall follow out his contention (35).

If I find an arrowhead in a field, I may start wondering why it exists. I can, as surcease for this particular wonder, come to find out about the Indian tribe that camped there a hundred or so years ago and made arrowheads. Yet I can in turn wonder about why these Indians existed and camped in that particular place at that particular time, and given a causally sufficient answer about that by specifying certain quite contingent states of affairs or beings, I can in turn wonder about why they existed. The same question can arise for any of the contingent realities I mention. I can always ask for the causally sufficient reasons for the existence of any

132

such beings, events or states of affairs. Where such contingent realities are involved, we can continue indefinitely to ask such questions.

However, in looking for a *final* answer, i.e. an answer 'which puts an end to the indefinitely long series of questions and answers where the answer to each question mentions a being or state of affairs about which precisely the same question may be asked', we are looking for a statement which legitimately 'puts an end to the series of questions and answers and allows no further question of the same sort' (36). To speak of God — to say all things are referred to God and depend on God — is to give such an answer, for it is a conceptual blunder of the first order to ask why does God exist or to ask for the state of affairs causally sufficient for God's existence. And this in effect indicates what is meant by speaking of God's necessity or God's non-contingency. A necessary being is a being about which one cannot sensibly ask why it exists. It is a being 'such that some statement referring to it can properly serve as a final answer to this sort of question and answer series . . . ' (37). We can conceptually identify God as that reality which is referred to in statements which make such a final answer. Moreover, this is surely no linguistic stipulation on Plantinga's part, for if we understand the language-games we play with 'God', we come to understand that we cannot sensibly ask: 'Why is it that God exists?' Indeed, if we believe that God exists, Plantinga argues, it is 'less than sensible to ask why he exists', because God is conceived of as uncreated and in no way causally dependent upon anything else. These remarks are grammatical remarks expressive of analytic truths, e.g. 'God is uncreated' is like 'Puppies are young'. Thus we cannot sensibly ask for the causally sufficient conditions for God's existence, for it is a logical impossibility that God should be in any way dependent on anything else. So it is clear that it is 'absurd to ask why God exists?' In this way, God's existence is necessary and in this way 'God' signifies a distinctive kind of reality — a reality utterly distinct from contingent reality.

I have now explicated the kind of *sui generis* reality that is being talked about when we speak of God, and we have made it evident, if such an argument is correct, that we are not talking nonsense when we speak of God, for God, after all, can be identified, though the identification must be conceptual. We have made evident the contrast between his kind of reality and the reality of contingent things, i.e. the reality of existents among other existents of the same order. If there is such a reality or reality as that which is referred to in giving a final answer in a question and answer series — an answer which finally puts an end to the series — then God exists; if not, not. But the point is — a point Plantinga utterly fails to meet — we do not know whether or not there is or even logically could be such an answer. Statements using the word 'God' or synonymous cognate expressions will not do for such final answers, for while we cannot sensibly ask 'Why does God exist?', since God by definition has no cause, we can and do, if we understand what we are about, ask in such a series of questions and answers, 'Does "God" or "uncaused being" or "Maker of heaven and earth" really stand for or answer to a reality or reality at all or is it merely a confused idea?' We cannot ask 'Why does God exist?' but we can and do ask 'Is there a god?' or 'Are there divine realities?' or 'Is there an uncreated maker of heaven and earth? or 'Is there an absolutely independent being?' Such questions are in our series of questions and answers, and indeed are asked by believer and non-believer alike, and Plantinga has done nothing at all to show that these natural questions are in any way illegitimate or not part of the series of questions and answers arising out of questions concerning why certain natural phenomena exist or events occur. Since this is so, we are still quite at sea about what if anything could count as a final answer in such a question and answer series. We know negatively that it is something of which it is senseless to ask for its causally sufficient conditions, but here we are again back to a purely negative characterisation. We do not understand in any positive manner what we are talking about. We are no more able to 'conceptually identify' God than we are able to empirically or experientially identify him.

Conclusion

The thrust of this essay has been sceptical, indeed, atheistic. Judaism and Christianity make putative truth-claims, but I have tried to establish that their central claims remain just *putative* truth-claims. That they are actually without truth-value does not mean that they are meaningless. On the contrary, religious talk, it is generally agreed, is not flatly meaningless. There are deviant and non-deviant religious utterances. But for all that, it remains the case that such utterances as 'God created man in his image and likeness' or even 'There is a transcendent cause of the universe' or 'The universe is dependent on God' have no ascertainable truth-value, and we do not know what we are referring to when we use 'God' in a religiously appropriate way. The central concepts of God-talk do not appear to be sufficiently coherent to make Jewish-Christian-Islamic beliefs reasonable options. Thus, if my argument has been correct, not even moderate fideism is a defensible position: that is to say, it is not true that the admittedly mysterious and problematic concept of God has sufficient intelligibility and coherence to provide the foundation for a confessional group which is worthy of one's allegiance. This is not, I have argued, a bit of philosophical mythology but a conclusion drawn from a careful conceptual analysis of Jewish and Christian religious discourse.

If such a critique is in the main correct, it provokes (or should provoke) a very profound human crisis for many people in our culture. For while secularisation has dug deep, it remains in the main true that the characteristic attitudes linked with the Judaeo-Christian view of the world are so much a part of many people's lives that they are not easily abandoned for an utterly secular view of the world. Secularisation is natural given the conditions of contemporary life for most people, but it has trailing behind it a largely ornamental though still compulsively insisted-on religious staging rather than a secularist one. Secularisation indeed does not imply secularism. And the human toll resulting from a loss of faith should not be minimised. There are indeed people who very much need to believe. But it is also a fact that many individuals in our culture and other cultures as well have learned to live meaningful and humanly significant lives without any religious orientation, and it is also true that there are whole cultures which have remained at least as viable as our culture (though hardly so powerful) even though their religious faithful have had no belief at all in a Divine Creator. Moreover, there is no theoretical reason why we should try to base moral beliefs on religious ones. The starvation and degradation of people remain evil whether or not there is a god; honesty, understanding, truth, development of one's personality remain humanly speaking indispensable whether there is or is not a god. We need an orientation in life in virtue of which life can become significant. But we do not need a belief in God for that. Since this is so, there is no need to cling, as did Pascal or Kierkegaard, to a belief in God no matter what. Life makes sense in a godless world, or, rather, it makes as much sense or as little sense as it does in a Jewish, Christian or Islamic world. That there are those who do not feel this way — that there are those who would despair or suffer alienation with the loss of religious belief — attests to the psychological power of religious belief, but it does not show that their despair or alienation is justified or rational. A cool, non-evasive inspection of the grounds of morality and an honest review of what is necessary to give us a sense of the significance of life show that such despair and alienation are quite without warrant.

The core issue, thus, remains essentially intellectual: Is belief in God and a commitment to Judaism, Christianity or Islam justified or even reasonable? If the central arguments of this book have been near to their mark, if the fundamental contemporary critiques of religion I have elucidated and defended are well taken, then the answer must be that such a religious belief or commitment is not even reasonable, let alone justified.

Notes

CHAPTER 1

1. Alasdair MacIntyre, 'Christianity and Marxism', p. 110. Sigmund Freud, 'The Future of an Illusion', pp. 65-6. (For full publishing details, see Select Bibliography.)

2. I have tried, in my 'Ethics Without God' and 'Linguistic Philosophy and the Meaning of Life', in 'Cross-Currents', xiv 3 (summer 1964), to come to grips with that problem.

3. John Hick, 'The Justification of Religious Belief', in 'Theology', lxxi (Mar 1969) 106.

4. Bernard Williams, 'Has "God" a Meaning?', in 'Question' i (Feb 1968) 51.

5. Ludwig Wittgenstein, 'Tractatus Logico-Philosophicus', 4.024.

6. D. Z. Phillips, 'The Concept of Prayer'.

7. Hugo Meynell has shown how such reductionism works for such philosophers as Kant, Schleiermacher, Hegel and Braithwaite in his 'Sense, Nonsense and Christianity'. But J. C. Thornton, in 'Religious Belief and "Reductionism" ', in 'Sophia', v (Oct 1966), has raised important questions about reductionism.

8. Kai Nielsen, 'Wittgensteinian Fideism', in 'Philosophy', xlii (July 1967) and 'Language and the Concept of God', in 'Question' (Jan 1969).

9. D. Z. Phillips, 'The Concept of Prayer', p. 10.

10. Ibid., p. 11.

11. J. M. Cameron, 'Is There Hope for Religion?', in 'New York Review of Books', xii 7 (Apr 1969) 31.

12. Terence Penelhum, 'Logic and Theology', in 'Canadian Journal of Theology', iv (1958) 258.

13. D. Z. Phillips, 'Faith and Philosophy', in 'Universities Quarterly' (Mar 1967) p. 239.

14. Ibid., p. 240.

15. Ibid.

16. Ibid.

17. Ibid.

18. Ibid., p. 241.

19. Ibid.

20. Ibid.

21. Dom Joseph Coombe-Tennant in his 'Sceptics and Believers', in 'Downside Review', lxxxiii (1965), makes evident how important it is to come to grips with these issues.

22. Donald Evans, 'Commentary on Paul Edwards' Paper', in Edward H. Madden, R. Handy and Marvin Forber (eds), 'The Idea of God', has raised questions about such distinctions.

23. N. H. G. Robinson, 'Faith and Truth', in 'Scottish Journal of Theology', xix (June 1966) 157.

24. For such discussions of the problem of evil, see John Hick, 'Evil and the God of Love', Alvin Plantinga, 'God and Other Minds', and D. Z. Phillips, 'The Concept of Prayer'.

CHAPTER 2

1. Herman Tennesen's 'Happiness Is for Pigs', in 'Journal of Existentialism', vii, 26 (winter 1966—7) 200.

2. John Bowden and James Richmond (eds), 'A Reader in Contemporary Theology', p. 18.

3. John Passmore discusses this 'existence-monism' in his 'Philosophical Reasoning'.

4. A. J. Ayer, 'What I Believe', in 'What I Believe', p. 13.

5. Ninian Smart, 'Theology, Philosophy, and the Natural Sciences' (Birmingham, 1962).

6. A. J. Ayer (ed.), 'Logical Positivism', p.11.

7. A. J. Ayer, 'The Vienna Circle', in 'The Revolution in Philosophy', p. 74.

8. Ibid.

9. H. H. Price, 'Logical Positivism and Theology', in 'Philosophy', x (Sep 1935), R. B. Braithwaite, 'An Empiricist's View of the Nature of Religious Belief', and

Antony Flew, 'Theology and Falsification', the last two are both reprinted in John Hick (ed.), 'The Existence of God'.

10. In the introduction to a recent anthology, Ronald E. Santoni (ed.), 'Religious Language and the Problem of Religious Knowledge', it has been called 'brash and arbitrary' (p. 18). See also p. 30.

11. Norman Malcolm has done this in his 'Anselm's Ontological Arguments', reprinted in John Hick (ed.), 'The Existence of God', and Alvin Plantinga, while not subscribing to any of the 'proofs', has argued powerfully against many of the traditional 'knockout' refutations of them. See Alvin Plantinga, 'God and Other Minds'.

12. See A. MacIntyre in his 'Difficulties in Christian Belief' and in his 'The Logical Status of Religious Belief' in Stephen Toulmin et al. (eds), 'Metaphysical Beliefs' (S.C.M. Press, 1957). Since writing these, MacIntyre has radically changed his position. See his 'The Debate About God: Victorian Relevance and Contemporary Irrelevance', in Alasdair MacIntyre and Paul Ricoeur (eds), 'The Religious Significance of Atheism'.

13. See John Hick, 'Faith and Knowledge', and Diogenes Allen, 'The Reasonableness of Faith'. I do not mean to suggest that Hick and Allen have identical positions, for there are certainly important differences between them. But in the general sense characterised in the text they are both fideists.

14. Braithwaite, op. cit., p. 230.

15. Ibid.

16. A. J. Ayer, 'Language, Truth and Logic', 2nd ed. (Victor Gollancz, 1946) p. 116.

17. A. J. Ayer (ed.), 'Logical Positivism', p. 11.

18. Price, op. cit., pp. 327–8.

19. A. J. Ayer (ed.), Logical Positivism', p. 12.

20. Price, op. cit., p. 321.

21. Ibid., p. 329.

22. Ibid., p. 327.

23. Ibid., p. 319.

24. Ibid., p. 320.

25. Ibid., p. 331.

26. Ibid., pp. 331–2.

27. Braithwaite, op. cit., p. 231.

28. Ibid., p. 231.

29. Ibid., p. 232.

30. Ibid.

31. Ibid.

32. Ibid.

33. Antony Flew, 'Theology and Falsification', in A. Flew and A. MacIntyre (eds), 'New Essays in Philosophical Theology', pp. 96—7. Note as well the essays by J. Kellenberger, T. McPherson and Antony Flew in 'Religious Studies', v 1 (Oct 1969).

34. Flew, op. cit. p. 98.

35. Ibid.

36. Ibid.

37. Braithwaite, op. cit., p. 234. With reference to the present context a case for so construing religious utterances has been interestingly made by B. C. Clarke, 'Linguistic Analysis and the Philosophy of Religion', in 'Monist', xlvii (spring 1963), but in turn this interesting argument has been decisively refuted by Adel Daher, 'God and Logical Necessity' in 'Philosophical Studies', xviii (National University of Ireland, 1969).

38. Ibid.

39. Ibid.

40. Price, op. cit., p. 320.

41. See here Rush Rhees, 'Without Answers' (Routledge & Kegan Paul, 1969) pp. 114, 126—32.

42. Smart, op. cit., p. 8.

43. John Passmore, 'Christianity and Positivism', in ('Australasian Journal of Philosophy', xxxv (1957).

44. Price, op. cit., p. 330.

45. Kai Nielsen, 'On Speaking of God', in 'Theoria', xxviii, 2 (1962), and 'The Quest for God' (Harper & Row, forthcoming).

46. Flew, op. cit., p. 98.

CHAPTER 3

1. John Passmore, 'Christianity and Positivism', in 'Australasian Journal of Philosophy', xxxv (1956), and

140

J. O. Urmson, 'Philosophical Analysis' (Oxford University Press, 1956).

2. H. H. Price, 'Logical Positivism and Theology', in 'Philosophy', x (Sep 1935) 315.

3. J. L. Evans, 'The Foundations of Empiricism', p. 14.

4. Ibid.

5. A. J. Ayer, 'Language, Truth and Logic', 2nd ed., p. 16.

6. E. L. Mascall, 'Words and Images', p. 12.

7. Ibid.

8. Ibid.

9. Ayer has done this in his BBC debate with Father Copleston (1949), reprinted in A. Pap and P. Edwards, 'A Modern Introduction to Philosophy', as 'Logical Positivism: A Debate', and in his discussion of the Vienna Circle (1956) in 'The Revolution in Philosophy' and in his introduction to an anthology, 'Logical Positivism', edited by Ayer.

10. Mascall, op. cit., p. 13.

11. A. J. Ayer, 'Logical Positivism: A Debate' in A. Pap and Paul Edwards, 'A Modern Introduction to Philosophy', pp. 742–3.

12. Ibid., p. 745.

13. Ibid., p. 755.

14. Ibid., p. 748.

15. Note also his remarks in his 'The Vienna Circle', in 'The Revolution in Philosophy', pp. 74–5.

16. A. J. Ayer, 'Introduction' to his 'Logical Positivism', pp. 15–16.

17. All references to E. L. Mascall's 'Words and Images' are to chap 1.

18. A. J. Ayer, 'Logical Positivism: A Debate', in A. Pap and Paul Edwards, 'A Modern Introduction to Philosophy', p. 743.

19. A. J. Ayer, 'Language, Truth and Logic', p. 115.

20. Ibid., p. 116.

21. Ibid., p. 118.

22. Mascall, op. cit., p. 12.

23. Ibid.

24. A. J. Ayer, 'Logical Positivism: A Debate', in A. Pap and P. Edwards, 'A Modern Introduction to Philosophy'. p. 743.

25. Mascall, op. cit., p. 12.

26. Ibid.

27. Ibid.

28. W. T. Stace, 'Mysticism and Philosophy', and Ninian Smart, 'Mystical Experience', in 'Sophia', i 1 (Apr 1962) and 'Interpretation and Mystical Experience', in 'Religious Studies', i 1 (1965).

29 J. N. Findlay, 'The Logic of Mysticism', in 'Religious Studies', ii (Apr 1967) 156–67.

30. Ninian Smart, 'Interpretation and Mystical Experience', in 'Religious Studies', i (Apr 1965) 85.

31. Ibid.

CHAPTER 4

1. George Mavrodes, in a book review, 'Journal of Philosophy', lxii (27 May 1965).

2. Alvin Plantinga, 'God and Other Minds', p. 168.

3. Ibid., p. 167.

4. This is in reality disingenuous of Plantinga, for he read through the relevant sections of William Alston's anthology, 'Religious Belief and Philosophical Thought', and Alston quite clearly and simply states what the challenge comes to there. See William Alston (ed.), 'Religious Belief and Philosophical Thought', pp. 224–5.

5. Plantinga, op. cit., p. 168.

6. This presupposition is accepted by Plantinga. For some defences of this presupposition, see John Hick, 'Christianity', in Paul Edwards (ed.), 'The Encyclopedia of Philosophy', ii 104–8, and Anthony Ralls, 'Ontological Presupposition in Religion', in 'Sophia' (Apr 1964) p. 8.

7. Kai Nielsen, 'On Fixing the Reference Range of God', in 'Religious Studies', ii (Oct 1966) 16.

8. Plantinga, op. cit., p. 162. Kai Nielsen, 'God and Verification Again', in 'Canadian Journal of Theology', xi 2 (1965) 135–41.

9. Stephen Toulmin, 'The Uses of Argument' (Cambridge University Press, 1958).

10. Plantinga, op. cit., p. 163.

11. Paul R. Clifford's ('The Factual Reference of Theological Assertions', in Religious Studies, iii (Oct 1967) 339—46) criticism of me assumes, quite gratuitously, that I am defending such a criterion, and since the whole of his criticism turns on this point it is without force.

12. That this is so is evident in his debate with Copleston and he also explicitly states it in his introduction to the volume 'Logical Positivism', p. 14.

13. D. Z. Phillips, 'The Concept of Prayer',

14. This point of view is well defended by Diogenes Allen, 'The Reasonableness of Faith'. But see my review in 'Theology Today' (Oct 1969).

15. It is not that I am maintaining that if no simple observation statement taken by itself is incompatible with 'God governs the world', then this religious proposition is devoid of factual significance. This is much too strong. (See here George Mavrodes' book review, 'Journal of Philosophy, lxii (27 May 1965). But I am maintaining that such a statement and such observation statements, taken in *a discourse* in conjunction with other statements, must indicate through the observation statements of that discourse, some differential experience which is relevant to the truth or falsity of the religious proposition if it is to have factual significance.

16. Plantinga, op. cit., p. 167.

17. Ibid.

18. Ibid., p. 168.

19. A. J. Ayer and F. C. Copleston, 'Logical Positivism: A Debate', in Paul Adwards and Arthur Pap (eds) 'A Modern Introduction to Philosophy', 2nd ed., pp. 754—5.

20. Ibid., p. 754.

21. Robert Coburn, 'A Budget of Theological Puzzles', in 'Journal of Religion', xliii (Apr 1963) 89—90.

22. Bernard Williams, 'Tertullian's Paradox', in A. Flew and A. MacIntyre (eds), 'New Essays in Philosophical Theology', pp. 187—211, and Kai Nielsen, 'Can Faith Validate God-talk?' in Martin Marty and Dean Peerman (eds), 'New Theology', no. 1.

23. William Alston, 'Philosophy of Language', pp. 62-83.

24. John Wisdom, 'Paradox and Discovery', p. 49.

25. Perry Anderson, 'Components of the National Culture', in 'New Left Review', 1 (1968) 22. See also C. K. Grant, 'Belief and Action' p. 3.

26. Ian Crombie, 'Theology and Falsification', in A. Flew and A. MacIntyre (eds), 'New Essays in Philosophical Theology' (1955), and 'The Possibility of Theological Statements', in B. Mitchell (ed.), 'Faith and Logic' (1957). John Hick, 'Faith and Knowledge', 2nd ed. (Ithaca, 1966), John Hick, 'Philosophy of Religion' (New York, 1962), 'Comment on Luther J. Binkley's "What Characterizes Religious Language?"', in 'Journal for the Scientific Study of Religion', ii 1 (fall 1962), 'A Comment on Professor Binkley's Reply', in 'Journal for the Scientific Study of Religion', ii 2 (spring 1963), 'Religious Faith as Experiencing-as', in 'Talk of God', Royal Institute of Philosophy Lectures, vol. 2 (1967—8).

27. Kai Nielsen, 'Eschatological Verification', in 'Canadian Journal of Theology', ix 4 (1963), and Kai Nielsen, 'On Fixing the Reference Range of "God"', in 'Religious Studies', ii 1 (1966).

28. John Hick, 'Faith and Knowledge', 2nd ed. (Ithaca, 1966) pp. 196—9.

29. Ibid., p. 195.

30. Ibid., pp. 124, 169.

31. Ibid., pp. 169, 195. See also his discussion with Binkley cited in note 26.

32. Ibid., p. 90.

33. Ibid., p. 169.

34. Ibid., p. 178.

35. William Bean, 'Eschatological Verification: Fortress or Fairyland', in 'Methodos', xvi, 69 (1964).

36. John Hick, 'Faith and Knowledge', 2nd ed., p. 186.

37. Ibid., p. 187.

38. Ibid.

39. Ibid.

40. Ibid., p. 188.

41. Ibid., p. 189. Italics mine.

42. Ibid., p. 189.

43. Ibid., pp. 189—90.

44. Ibid., p. 190.

45. Ibid., p. 191.

46. Ibid.

47. This conception was suggested to me by Terence Penelhum's related but distinct conception of a 'theistic statement'. See Terence Penelhum, 'Is a Religious Epistemology Possible?', in 'Knowledge and Necessity', Royal Institute of Philosophy Lectures, vol. 3 (1968–9) p. 264.

48. Ibid., p. 274.

49. Kai Nielsen, 'Eschatological Verification', in 'Canadian Journal of Theology', ix 4 (1963).

50. John Hick, 'Faith and Knowledge', 2nd ed., pp. 196–9.

51. Ibid., pp. 190–1.

52. Ibid., p. 193.

53. Ibid., p. 197 (italics mine).

54. Ibid., p. 198.

55. Mary Hesse, 'Talk of God', in 'Philosophy', xliv 170 (Oct 1969).

56. John Hick, 'Religious Faith as Experiencing–as', in 'Talk of God', Royal Institute of Philosophy Lectures, vol. 2 (1967–8).

57. Wilfrid Sellars, 'Science and Metaphysics' (1968). See also Richard Rorty's discussion of this book in 'Philosophy', xlv 171 (Jan 1970) 66–70.

58. Sellars, op. cit., p. 83.

59. Ibid., pp.101–2.

60. John Hick, 'Religious Faith as Experiencing–as', in 'Talk of God', pp. 20–35.

61. Ibid. For an argument with similar conclusions to Hick's see John F. Miller, 'Science and Religion: Their Logical Similarity', in 'Religious Studies', iii 1 (Oct 1969).

62. John Hick, 'Religious Faith as Experiencing-as', in 'Talk of God', p.23

63. Mary Hesse, op. cit., and John F. Miller, op. cit.

64. John Hick, 'Religious Faith as Experiencing-as', in 'Talk of God', p.26.

65. Ibid., p. 30.

66. Ibid., p. 26.

67. Sellars, op. cit., p. ix.

68. Ibid., p. 13.

69. Ibid., pp. 139–40.

CHAPTER 5

1. Jerry H. Gill, 'God-Talk: Getting on With It', in 'Southern Journal of Philosophy', vi 2 (summer 1968) 115–24.

2. A. J. Ayer, 'What I Believe', in 'What I Believe' (1966) p. 13.

3. N. Clarke, 'It Is Compatible', in John Hick (ed.), 'Faith and the Philosophers', p. 142. A philosopher of a Wittgensteinian persuasion might counter that Father Clarke's remark is meta-theological and not a part of any form of life to which we should extend linguistic tolerances. Conceptual relativists (e.g. Wilfrid Sellars) of a more formalist persuasion would not so argue, but would count a theological or philosophical system as a linguistic framework. Yet it should be replied to such Wittgensteinians that Clarke's remark certainly does not appear meta-linguistic and there is no reason to think that was his intent. But even if it is a disguised meta-linguistic statement in the material mode, it still would be easy enough to take a plain religious statement such as 'God created the heavens and the earth' and make the same argument as the argument I made above.

4. D. Z. Phillips's work is paradigmatic here. See his 'The Concept of Prayer' and his introduction and essays in D. Z. Phillips (ed.), 'Religion and Understanding'.

5. John Wisdom, 'Paradox and Discovery', particularly essays i and v, and in his 'Philosophy and Psychoanalysis', (Oxford: Blackwell, 1953) pp. 149–68.

6. Though there is something that tentatively and not very convincingly moves in that direction in Alasdair MacIntyre's 'Is Understanding Religion Compatible with Believing?', in John Hick (ed.), 'Faith and the Philosophers', pp. 115-33.

7. Peter Winch, 'Understanding A Primitive Society', in D. Z. Phillips (ed.), 'Religion and Understanding', p. 13.

8. D. Z. Phillips, 'The Concept of Prayer', p. 9.

9. Ibid.

10. Winch, op. cit., pp. 35–42.

11. D. Z. Phillips, 'The Concept of Prayer', p. 130.

12. There are those who would wish to counter what I have argued here concerning such a religious utterance as

'Christ is the truth and the way'. They would agree that if conceptual relativism is true such utterances cannot be reasonably asserted in a competitive way with the claims of other forms of life. But realising its full relativity, a man might make his claim for Christ all the same. But he need not assume, as I assume he does, that in making such a claim he must assume that Christ is the truth and the way holds for all men everywhere. Christian-talk, of which such a claim is a part, is learned at an early age when all men in their cultural diversity are not even something that the participants in this discourse have any understanding of. With such a small acquaintance with men of other cultures and their circumstances, how could they be making such a claim? Since this is so, I cannot, it could be argued, correctly claim that the Christian thinks he is making a claim for all men. But why not? There is the pervasive anthropological phenomenon of ethnocentricism, and confusion is not a rare phenomenon. People typically assume that their ways are the right ways for them and for everyone else as well and they, without knowing very much about others, assume that either they will or ideally should believe as they do. The very choice of '*the* way' and '*the* truth' in 'Christ is the truth and the way' indicates that such a confused and indeed arrogant assumption is operating.

13. Peter Winch, 'The Idea of a Social Science', p. 100.

14. Peter Winch, 'On Understanding a Primitive Society', in 'Religion and Understanding', p. 28.

15. D. Z. Phillips, 'Subjectivity and Religious Truth in Kierkegaard', in 'Sophia' (1968) and Kai Nielsen, 'Language and the Concept of God', in 'Question', ii (Jan 1969).

16. Norman Malcolm, 'Is it a Religious Belief that "God Exists"?', in John Hick (ed.), 'Faith and the Philosophers', pp. 103–10, and Kai Nielsen, 'On Believing that God Exists', in 'Southern Journal of Philosophy', v (fall 1967).

17. D. Z. Phillips, 'The Concept of Prayer', p. 100.

18. John Wisdom, 'Paradox and Discovery', pp. 49–56.

CHAPTER 6

1. See my 'Wittgensteinian Fideism', in 'Philosophy', xlii (July 1967) and chaps v, vi and vii of my 'Quest For God'.

2. J. N. Findlay, 'Can God's Existence be Disproved?', In A. Flew and A. MacIntyre (eds), 'New Essays in Philosophical Theology'; Paul Edwards, 'Difficulties in the Idea of God', in Edward H. Madden, Rollo Handy, and Marvin Farber (eds), 'The Idea of God'; Ronald Hepburn, 'Poetry and Religious Belief', in Stephen Toulmin et al. (eds), 'Metaphysical Beliefs'; and Kai Nielsen, 'In Defense of Atheism', in Howard Kiefer and Milton Munitz (eds), 'Perspectives in Education, Religion and the Arts'.

3. Ronald Hepburn, 'From World to God', in 'Mind', lxxii (1963) 50.

4. Antony Flew, 'God and Philosophy', p. 31.

5. Edwards, op. cit., p. 45. See also Peter Geach, 'God and the Soul' (Routledge & Kegan Paul, 1969) pp. 16–17.

6. Edwards, op. cit., p. 48.

7. Flew, op. cit., p. 44.

8. Ibid., p. 47.

9. C. J. F. Williams, review of 'God and Philosophy', in 'Downside Review', lxxxv (Jan 1967) 77.

10. Donald Evans, 'Commentary on Paul Edwards' Paper', in Edward H. Madden, Rollo Handy and Marvin Farver (eds), 'The Idea of God', and Alasdair MacIntyre, 'A Kind of Atheism', in the 'Guardian' (July 1966).

11. Evans, op. cit., and W. D. Hudson, 'Ludwig Wittgenstein', pp. 33–41.

12. Hudson, op. cit., p. 40.

13. Ibid., p. 40.

14. Edwards, op. cit., p. 93.

15. Hudson, op. cit., p. 39.

16. Ibid.

17. Ibid.

18. Ibid., p. 40.

19. Ibid.

20. Ibid., p. 39.

21. Evans, op. cit., p. 84.

22. Hudson, op. cit., p. 36; Peter Geach, op. cit., pp.

23. Paul Edwards, 'Reply to Commentators', in 'The Idea of God', p. 95.

24. Ibid., p. 95.

25. Flew, op. cit., p. 24.

26. Ibid., p. 24.

27. Ibid., pp. 25, 42—3.

28. Ibid., p. 31.

29. Ibid., p. 32.

30. Ibid.

31. Ibid., p. 32.

32. Ibid., p. 34.

33. Ibid., p. 32.

34. D. Z. Phillips, 'Philosophy, Theology and The Reality of God', in 'Philosophical Quarterly', xiii (1963) 345.

35. Alvin Plantinga, 'God And Other Minds', pp.181—3.

36. Ibid., p. 181.

37. Ibid.

Select Bibliography

Anthologies and Collections containing
Critical Discussions of Religion

William Alston, (ed.), 'Religious Belief and Philosophical Thought' (New York: Harcourt Brace, 1963).

ArthurJ. Bellinzoni, Jr, and Thomas V. Litzenburg, Jr (eds), Intellectual Honesty and Religious Commitment' (Philadelphia: Fortress Press, 1969).

William Blackstone (ed.), 'Problems of Religious Knowledge and Language' (Athens, Ga: University of Georgia Press, 1971).

John Bowden and James Richmond (eds), 'A Reader in Contemporary Theology' (S.C.M. Press, 1967).

British Broadcasting Corporation, 'Religion and Humanism' (1964).

Steven M. Cahn (ed.), 'Philosophy of Religion' (New York: Harper & Row, 1970).

Antony Flew and Alasdair MacIntyre (eds), 'New Essays in Philosophical Theology' (New York: Macmillan 1955).

Jerry A. Gill (ed.), 'Philosophy and Religion: Some Contemporary Perspectives' (Minneapolis, Minn.: Burgess publishing Company, 1968).

John Hick (ed.), 'Classical and Contemporary Readings on the Philosophy of Religion' (Englewood Cliffs, N.J.: Prentice-Hall, 1964).

— (ed.), 'The Existence of God' (New York: Macmillan, 1964).

— (ed.), 'Faith and the Philosophers' (New York: St Martin's Press, 1964).

Dallas M. High (ed.), 'New Essays on Religious Language' (New York: Oxford University Press, 1969).

Sidney Hook (ed.), 'Religious Experience and Truth' (New York: New York University Press, 1961).

Howard Kiefer and Milton Munitz (eds), 'Perspectives in Education, Religion and the Arts' (New York: State

University of New York Press, 1970).

Alasdair MacIntyre (ed.), 'Metaphysical Beliefs' (S.C.M. Press, 1957).

— and Paul Ricoeur (eds.), 'The Religious Significance of Atheism' (New York: Columbia University Press, 1969).

Edward H. Madden, Rollo Handy and Marvin Farber (eds), 'The Idea of God' (Springfield, Ill: Charles Thomas, 1968).

George I. Mavrodes (ed.), 'Rationality of Belief in God' (Englewood Cliffs, N.J.: Prentice-Hall, 1970).

Basil Mitchell (ed.), 'Faith and Logic' (Allen & Unwin, 1957).

D. Z. Phillips (ed.), 'Religion and Understanding' (Oxford: Blackwell, 1967).

Nelson Pike (ed.), 'God and Evil' (Englewood Cliffs, N.J.: Prentice-Hall, 1965).

Royal Institute of Philosophy Lectures, vol. 2, 'Talk of God' (Macmillan, 1969).

Ronald E. Santoni (ed.), 'Religious Language and the Problem of Religious Knowledge' (Bloomington, Ind.: Indiana University Press, 1968).

Nineteenth-century Background

Ludwig Feuerbach, 'The Essence of Christianity', trans. George Eliot (New York: Harper & Row, 1957).

Sir William Hamilton, 'Philosophy of the Unconditioned', in 'Edinburgh Review' (1829).

John Holloway, 'The Victorian Sage' (Archon Books, 1962).

T. H. Huxley, 'Collected Essays', vol. v (Macmillan, 1894).

Eugene Kamenka, 'The Philosophy of Ludwig Feuerbach' (Routledge & Kegan Paul, 1970).

Søren Kierkegaard, 'Concluding Unscientific Postscript', trans. D. F. Swenson and W. Lowrie (Princeton, N.J.: Princeton University Press, 1941).

Alasdair MacIntyre, 'Secularization and Moral Change' (Oxford University Press, 1967).

— , 'Christianity and Marxism' (New York: Schocken Books, 1969).

H. L. Mansel, 'The Limits of Religious Thought', 5th ed. (Murray, 1867).

Karl Marx and Friedrich Engels, 'On Religion' (Moscow: Foreign Language Publications, 1950).

B. M. G. Reardon, 'The Theological Atheist: A Reassessment of Ludwig Feuerbach', in 'The Listener', 11 Jan 1963).
— (ed.), 'Religious Thought in the Nineteenth Century' (Cambridge University Press, 1966).
Leslie Stephen, 'An Agnostic's Apology and Other Essays' (Smith, Elder, 1893).
Basil Willey, 'Nineteenth Century Studies' (Chatto & Windus, 1949).

Twentieth-century Critiques and Counter-critiques

I. Books

Diogenes Allen, 'The Reasonableness of Faith' (Washington and Cleveland: Corpus Books, 1968).
William Alston, 'Philosophy of Language' (Englewood Cliffs, N.J.: Prentice-Hall, 1964).
A. J. Ayer (ed.), 'Logical Positivism' (Allen & Unwin, 1959).
— (ed.), 'The Revolution in Philosophy' (Macmillan, 1961).
— (ed.), 'What I Believe' (Allen & Unwin, 1966).
William Blackstone, 'The Problem of Religious Knowledge' (Englewood Cliffs, N.J.: Prentice-Hall, 1963).
Stuart C. Brown, 'Do Religious Claims Make Sense?' (S.C.M. Press, 1969).
William A. Christian, 'Meaning and Truth in Religion' (Princeton, N.J.: Princeton University Press, 1964).
C. J. Ducasse, 'A Philosophical Scrutiny of Religion' (New York: Ronald Press, 1953).
Donald D. Evans, 'The Logic of Self-Involvement: A Philosophical Study of Everyday Language with Special Reference to the Christian Use of Language About God as Creator' (S.C.M. Press, 1963).
J. L. Evans, 'The Foundations of Empiricism' (Cardiff: 1965).
Frederick Ferré, 'Language, Logic and God' (Eyre & Spottiswoode, 1962).
Antony Flew, 'God and Philosophy' (Hutchinson, 1966).
Sigmund Freud, 'The Future of an Illusion', revised and edited by J. Strachey, trans. W. D. Robson-Scott (Hogarth Press and Institute of Psycho-Analysis, 1962).
A. Boyce Gibson, 'Theism and Empiricism' (S.C.M. Press,

1970).

Axel Hägerström, 'Philosophy and Religion' (Oxford: Blackwell, 1964).

Raeburne S. Heimbeck, 'Theology and Meaning' (Allen & Unwin, 1969).

Ronald Hepburn, 'Christianity and Paradox' (New York: Humanities Press, 1958).

John Hick, 'Philosophy of Religion' (Englewood Cliffs, N.J.: Prentice-Hall, 1963).

—, 'Evil and the God of Love' (New York: Harper & Row, 1966).

—, 'Faith and Knowledge', 2nd ed. (Ithaca, N.Y.: Cornell University Press, 1966).

Sidney Hook, 'The Quest for Being' (New York: St Martin's Press, 1961).

William Hordern, 'Speaking of God: Nature and Purpose of Theological Language' (New York: Macmillan 1964).

Walter Kaufmann, 'Critique of Religion and Philosophy' (New York: Harper & Row, 1958).

—, 'The Faith of a Heretic' (Garden City, N.J.: Doubleday, 1961).

John King-Farlow, 'Reason and Religion' (Toronto: Darton, Longman & Todd, 1970).

H. D. Lewis, 'Our Experience of God' (New York: Macmillan, 1959).

Alasdair MacIntyre, 'Difficulties in Christian Belief' (S.C.M. Press, 1959).

John Macquarrie, 'God-Talk' (S.C.M. Press, 1967).

C. B. Martin, 'Religious Belief' (Ithaca, N.Y.: Cornell University Press, 1965).

James A. Martin, 'The New Dialogue Between Philosophy and Theology' (London: Black; Greenwich, Conn.: Seabury Press, 1966).

E. L. Mascall, 'Words and Images' (Longmans, 1957).

Wallace I. Matson, 'The Existence of God' (Ithaca: Cornell University Press, 1965).

George Mavrodes, 'Belief in God, (New York: Random House, 1970).

Hugo Meynell, 'Sense, Nonsense and Christianity' (Sheed & Ward, 1966).

John Passmore, 'Philosophical Reasoning' (New York: Basic

Books, 1969).

D. Z. Phillips, 'The Concept of Prayer' (Routledge & Kegan Paul, 1965).

Alvin Plantinga, 'God and Other Minds' (Ithaca, N.Y.: Cornell University Press, 1967).

H. H. Price, 'Belief' (Allen & Unwin, 1969).

W. V. Quine, 'Ontological Relativity and Other Essays' (New York: Columbia University Press, 1969).

Ian T. Ramsey, 'Religious Language' (S.C.M. Press, 1957).

Rush Rhees, 'Without Answers' (Routledge & Kegan Paul, 1969).

James Richmond, 'Theology and Metaphysics' (S.C.M. Press, 1970).

James Ross, 'Philosophical Theology' (Indianapolis: Bobbs-Merrill, 1969).

Bertrand Russell, 'Why I Am Not a Christian: and Other Essays on Religion and Related Subjects', ed. P. Edwards (Allen & Unwin, 1957).

Paul F. Schmidt, 'Religious Knowledge' (Glencoe, Ill.: Free Press of Glencoe, 1961).

Wilfrid Sellars, 'Science, Perception and Reality' (Routledge & Kegan Paul, 1963).

— , 'Science and Metaphysics' (Routledge & Kegan Paul, 1968).

Ninian Smart, 'Philosophers and Religious Truth', 2nd ed. (New York: Macmillan, 1970).

W. T. Stace, 'Mysticism and Philosophy' (Philadelphia: Lippincott, 1960).

Peter Winch, 'The Idea of a Social Science' (Routledge & Kegan Paul, 1958).

John Wisdom, 'Paradox and Discovery' (Oxford: Blackwell, 1965).

Ludwig Wittgenstein, 'Philosophical Investigations', trans. G. E. M. Anscombe and R. Rhees, (Oxford: Blackwell, 1953).

Ludwig Wittgenstein, 'Tractatus Logico-Philosophicus', trans. D. Pears and B. McGuinness, (Routledge & Kegan Paul, 1961).

II. Articles and Essays

William Alston, 'Ineffability', in 'Philosophical Review', lxv (1956).

— , 'The Elucidation of Religious Statements', in William L. Reese and Eugene Freeman (eds), in 'Process and Divinity' (Lasalle, Ill.: Open Court Publishing Co., 1964).

R. W. Ashby, 'Verifiability Principle', in Paul Edwards, (ed.), 'The Encyclopedia of Philosophy', viii (New York: Macmillan, 1967).

A. J. Ayer and F. Copleston, 'Logical Positivism: A Debate', in A. Pap and P. Edwards (eds), 'A Modern Introduction to Philosophy' rev. ed. (New York: Free Press, 1965).

William Bean, 'Eschatological Verification: Fortress or Fairyland' in 'Methodos', xvi (1964).

Richard H. Bell, 'Wittgenstein and Descriptive Theology', in 'Religious Studies', v 1 (Oct 1969).

Luther J. Binkley, 'What Characterizes Religious Language?', in 'Journal for the Scientific Study of Religion', ii 1 (1962).

— , 'Reply to Professor Hick's Comment on "What Characterizes Religious Language?",' in 'Journal for the Scientific Study of Religion', ii (spring 1963).

Howard R. Burkle, 'Counting Against and Counting Decisively Against', in 'Journal of Religion', iv (1964).

J. M. Cameron, 'Is There Hope for Religion?' in 'New York Review of Books', xii 7 (Apr 1969).

B. Clark, 'Linguistic Analysis and the Philosophy of Religion', in 'Monist', xlvii 3 (spring 1963).

Paul R. Clifford, 'The Factual Reference of Theological Assertions', in 'Religious Studies', iii (Oct 1967).

Robert Coburn, 'A Budget of Theological Puzzles', in 'Journal of Religion' (Apr 1963).

Arthur B. Cody, 'On the Difference It Makes', in 'Inquiry', xii 4 (winter 1969).

Dom Joseph Coombe-Tennant, 'Sceptics and Believers', in 'Downside Review', lxxxiii (1965).

F. Copleston, S.J., 'Man, Transcendence and God', in 'Thought', xliii (1968).

Adel Daher, 'God and Logical Necessity', in 'Philosophical

Studies', xviii (National University of Ireland, 1969).

Malcolm L. Diamond, 'Contemporary Analysis: The Metaphysical Target and the Theological Victim', in 'Journal of Religion', xlvii 3 (July 1967).

D. Duff-Forbes, 'Theology and Falsification Again', in 'Australasian Journal of Philosophy', xxxix (1961) and Flew's reply, 'Falsification and Hypothesis in Theology', ibid., xl (1962) and Duff-Forbes's further reply in the same issue.

J. L. Evans, 'On Meaning and Verification', in 'Mind', lxii (1953).

Herbert Feigl, 'Is Science Relevant to Theology?', in 'Zygon', i 2 (June 1966).

J. N. Findlay, 'The Logic of Mysticism', in 'Religious Studies', ii (1967).

Richard Gale, 'Mysticism and Philosophy', in 'Journal of Philosophy', lvii (1960).

Jerry H. Gill, 'God-talk: Getting on With It', in 'Southern Journal of Philosophy', vi (summer 1968).

Paul Henle, 'Mysticism and Semantics', in 'Philosophy and Phenomenological Research', ix (1949).

Ronald Hepburn, 'From World to God', in 'Mind', lxxii (1963).

Mary Hesse, 'Talk of God', in 'Philosophy', xliv 170 (Oct 1969).

John Hick, 'Comment on Luther J. Binkley's "What Characterizes Religious Language?",' in 'Journal for the Scientific Study of Religion', ii 1 (fall 1962).

— , 'A Comment on Professor Binkley's Reply', in 'Journal for the Scientific Study of Religion', ii (spring 1963).

— , 'The Justification of Religious Belief', in 'Theology', lxxi (Mar 1968).

Robert Hoffman, 'Theistic Religion as Regression', in 'Insight', iv 3 (winter 1966).

Martin Hollis, 'Reason and Ritual', in 'Philosophy', xliii 165 (July 1968).

Paul L. Holmer, 'Language and Theology: Some Critical Notes', in 'Harvard Theological Review', lviii 3 (July 1965).

— , 'Atheism and Theism: A Comment on Academic Prejudice', in 'Lutheran World', xiii (1966).
156

W. D. Hudson, 'Transcendence', in 'Theology', lxix (Mar 1966).

J. R. Jones and D. Z. Phillips, 'Belief and Loss of Belief: A Discussion', in 'Sophia', ix 1 (Mar 1970).

Gordon Kaufman, 'Philosophy of Religion and Christian Theology', in 'Journal of Religion', xxxvii (Oct 1957).

Gordon Kaufman, 'On the Meaning of 'God'': Transcendence Without Mythology', in 'Harvard Theological Review', lix (Apr 1966).

J. Kellenberger, 'The Falsification Challenge', in 'Religious Studies', v 1 (Oct 1969); see also Flew's and Thomas McPherson's responses in the same issue.

E. D. Klemke, 'Are Religious Statements Meaningful?', in 'Journal of Religion', xlix (1960).

David Michael Levin, 'Reasons and Religious Belief', in 'Inquiry', xi 4 (winter 1969).

Colin Lyas, 'On the Coherence of Christian Atheism', in 'Philosophy', xlv 171 (Jan 1970).

P. J. McGrath, 'Professor Flew and the Stratonician Presumption', in 'Philosophical Studies', xviii (National University of Ireland, 1969).

Edward M. MacKinnon, S.J., 'Linguistic Analysis and the Transcendence of God', in 'Proceedings of the Twenty-third Annual Convention of the Catholic Theological Society of America', xxiii (17-20 June 1968, Washington, D.C.).

Paul Marhenke, 'The Criterion of Significance', in 'Proceedings and Addresses of the American Philosophical Association' (1950).

Gareth Matthews, 'Theology and Natural Theology', in 'Journal of Philosophy', lxi (1964).

George Mavrodes, 'God and Verification', in 'Canadian Journal of Theology', x (1964).

John F. Miller, 'Science and Religion: Their Logical Similarity', in 'Religious Studies', v 1 (Oct 1969).

Kai Nielsen, 'In Defense of Atheism', in Howard Kiefer and Milton Munitz (eds), 'Perspectives in Education, Religion and the Arts'.

—, 'Christian Positivism and the Appeal to Religious Experience', in 'Journal of Religion', xlii (Oct 1962).

—, 'Eschatological Verification', in 'Canadian Journal of

Theology', ix (1962).

— , 'God and Verification Again', in 'Canadian Journal of Theology', xi (1965).

— , 'On Fixing the Reference Range of "God",' in 'Religious Studies', ii 1 (1966).

— , 'Can Faith Validate God-talk?', in 'Theology Today', xx (1963).

— , 'Religious Perplexity and Faith', in 'Crane Review', viii (fall 1965).

— , 'Wittgensteinian Fideism', in 'Philosophy' xlii (July 1967).

— , 'The Primacy of Philosophical Theology', in 'Theology Today' (July 1970).

— , 'Language and the Concept of God', in 'Question', ii (Jan 1969).

— , 'On Speaking of God', in 'Theoria', xxviii, 2 (1962).

— , 'On Believing that God Exists', in 'Southern Journal of Philosophy', v (fall 1967).

Schubert M. Ogden, 'God and Philosophy: A Discussion with Antony Flew', in 'Journal of Religion', xlviii 2 (Apr 1968).

— , 'Theology and Metaphysics', in 'Criterion' (autumn 1969).

Humphrey Palmer, 'Understanding First', in 'Theology', lxxi 573 (Mar 1968).

John Passmore, 'Christianity and Positivism', in 'Australasian Journal of Philosophy', xxxv (1957).

Terence Penelhum, 'Logic and Theology', in 'Canadian Journal of Theology', iv (1958).

— , 'Is a Religious Epistemology Possible?', in 'Knowledge and Necessity', Royal Institute of Philosophy Lectures, vol. 3 (Macmillan, 1970).

D. Z. Phillips, 'Religious Belief and Philosophical Enquiry', in 'Theology', lxxi 573 (Mar 1968).

— , 'Philosophy, Theology and the Reality of God', in 'Philosophical Quarterly', xiii (1963).

— , 'Religious Beliefs and Language Games', in 'Ratio', xii (June 1970).

— , 'Faith and Philosophy', in 'Universities Quarterly' (Mar 1967).

— , 'Subjectivity and Religious Truth in Kierkegaard', in 'Sophia' (1968).

Vernon Pratt, 'The Inexplicable and the Supernatural', in 'Philosophy', xliii 165 (July 1968).

H. H. Price, 'Logical Positivism and Theology', in 'Philosophy', x (Sep 1935).

Anthony Ralls, 'Ontological Presupposition in Religion', in 'Sophia' (Apr 1964).

N. H. G. Robinson, 'Faith and Truth', in 'Scottish Journal of Theology', xix (June 1966).

Richard Rorty, 'Science and Metaphysics: Variations on Kantian Themes', in 'Philosophy', xlv 171 (Jan 1970).

Ninian Smart, 'Theology, Philosophy, and the Natural Sciences', Inaugural Lecture (University of Birmingham, 1962).

—, 'Mystical Experience', in 'Sophia', i no 1 (Apr 1962).

—, 'Interpretation and Mystical Experience', in 'Religious Studies', i no 1 (1965).

J. W. Swanson, 'Religious Discourse and Rational Preference Ranking', in 'American Philosophical Quarterly' (July 1967).

Herman Tennessen, 'Happiness Is for Pigs', in 'Journal of Existentialism', vii 26 (winter 1966-7).

J. C. Thornton, 'Religious Belief and "Reductionism",' in 'Sophia', v (Oct 1966).

James E. Tomberlin, 'Is Belief in God Justified?', in 'Journal of Philosophy', lxvii 2 (29 Jan 1970).

L. C. Velecky, 'Flew on Aquinas', in 'Philosophy', lxiii 165 (July 1968).

G. J. Warnock, 'Verification and the Use of Language', in 'Revue Internationale de Philosophie', xvii (1951).

Bernard Williams, 'Has "God" a Meaning?', in 'Question' i (Feb 1968).

This is but a sampling of the literature to be found in the journals. 'Sophia' and 'Religious Studies' are two particularly fertile sources of rigorous present-day philosophical theology. 'Theology', 'The Journal of Religion', 'The Scottish Journal of Theology', 'Theology Today', 'Zygon' 'The Journal for the Scientific Study of Religion', 'The Canadian Journal of Theology', while not so exclusively engaged in philosophical theology, also have articles devoted to philosophical theology. In addition, the philosophical journals sometimes have essays in philosophical theology. Note particularly 'Philosophy', 'Mind', 'Canadian Journal of Philosophy', 'Australasian Journal of Philosophy', 'Theoria', 'Inquiry', 'Philosophical Review', 'Philosophical Quarterly', 'American Philosophical Quarterly' and 'The International Philosophical Quarterly'.

Finally 'The Encyclopedia of Philosophy', ed. Paul Edwards (New York: Macmillan, 1967) and 'The Dictionary of the History of Ideas', ed. Philip P. Wiener (New York: Scribner's, 1971) have reliable articles on the philosophy of religion. In particular, note here the articles on 'Atheism', 'Agnosticism', 'Religion' (definitions of), 'Fideism', 'Skepticism', 'Logical Empiricism' and the 'Verifiability Principle'.

Index